Introvert-Friendly Careers: Jobs That Fit Your Personality

Shah Rukh

Published by Shah Rukh, 2024.

While every precaution has been taken in the preparation of this book, the publisher assumes no responsibility for errors or omissions, or for damages resulting from the use of the information contained herein.

INTROVERT-FRIENDLY CAREERS: JOBS THAT FIT YOUR PERSONALITY

First edition. June 4, 2024.

Copyright © 2024 Shah Rukh.

Written by Shah Rukh.

Table of Contents

Chapter 1: Understanding Introversion

Introversion is a personality trait that is often misunderstood and misrepresented in popular culture. To understand introversion comprehensively, it is essential to debunk common myths and highlight the realities of what it means to be an introvert.

One of the most pervasive myths about introverts is that they are shy or socially anxious. While some introverts may experience shyness or anxiety in social situations, these are not defining characteristics of introversion. Introversion is primarily about where a person derives their energy. Introverts tend to feel more energized and comfortable in solitary or low-stimulation environments, whereas extroverts gain energy from being around others. This difference in energy sources can manifest in various behaviors, but it is not synonymous with social anxiety.

Another myth is that introverts do not like people or are antisocial. In reality, introverts often enjoy social interactions, but they prefer deep, meaningful conversations over small talk and tend to thrive in one-on-one or small group settings rather than large gatherings. Introverts can form strong, lasting relationships and be very loyal friends. Their preference for quieter environments does not equate to a lack of social skills or a dislike of socializing. Rather, they may simply need time alone to recharge after social activities.

Introverts are sometimes perceived as lacking leadership qualities. This myth is rooted in the misconception that effective leaders must be outgoing and charismatic. However, introverts can be highly effective leaders. They often excel in listening, thoughtful decision-making, and building strong, supportive relationships with their team members. Many successful leaders, such as Bill Gates and Barack Obama, identify as introverts and have demonstrated that introversion can be an asset in leadership roles.

Another reality that dispels common myths is the introvert's capacity for creativity and focus. Introverts often have a rich inner life, spending much time reflecting and thinking deeply. This introspection can lead to high levels of creativity and innovation. Many artists, writers, scientists, and thinkers throughout history were introverts, using their inclination for solitary work to produce groundbreaking ideas and works of art. Their ability to concentrate deeply and work independently can lead to significant achievements in various fields.

The myth that introverts cannot thrive in social professions is also misleading. While introverts may not seek out social interaction in the same way extroverts do, they can still excel in careers that involve interacting with others. For instance, introverts can be excellent counselors, therapists, teachers, or doctors. In these roles, their ability to listen attentively, empathize, and provide thoughtful responses can be incredibly valuable. Introverts often create meaningful connections with those they work with, fostering trust and understanding.

In the workplace, introverts may be misunderstood as being disengaged or uninterested because they may not participate in discussions as vocally as their extroverted colleagues. However, this does not mean they are not contributing valuable ideas. Introverts often prefer to think before they speak, and their contributions can be thoughtful and insightful. Employers can benefit from creating environments where both introverts and extroverts can thrive, recognizing that introverts bring unique strengths to the table.

Another important reality is that introversion exists on a spectrum. Most people are not purely introverted or extroverted but exhibit traits of both to varying degrees. This concept, known as ambiversion, highlights that personality traits are fluid and context-dependent. Someone might display more introverted tendencies in one setting and more extroverted tendencies in another. Understanding this spectrum helps to appreciate the diversity of personalities and the strengths that different traits can bring to various situations.

The impact of societal norms on introverts should also be considered. Western cultures, particularly in the United States, often value extroverted traits such as assertiveness, sociability, and outgoingness. This can lead to introverts feeling pressured to conform to extroverted ideals, sometimes at the expense of their well-being. Recognizing and valuing introverted traits can lead to a more inclusive society where individuals feel comfortable being themselves and contributing their unique strengths.

Introverts also tend to excel in roles that require attention to detail and the ability to work independently. Jobs that involve research, writing, data analysis, and creative pursuits are often well-suited to introverts. Their ability to focus deeply and work methodically can lead to high-quality work and innovative solutions. For example, introverts can make excellent researchers, delving into complex topics with thoroughness and persistence. Writers and artists often find that their introspective nature allows them to explore and express ideas in profound and meaningful ways.

Understanding introversion involves recognizing the diversity and complexity of this personality trait. It requires debunking myths that portray introverts as shy, antisocial, or lacking in leadership qualities. Instead, it is essential to appreciate the strengths that introverts bring, such as their capacity for deep thinking, creativity, and meaningful social connections. By creating environments that value and support both introverted and extroverted traits, society can benefit from the full range of human potential. Recognizing that introversion and extroversion exist on a spectrum and that personality traits are fluid helps to foster a more inclusive and understanding world.

Chapter 2: Self-Assessment

Self-assessment is a critical process that enables individuals to understand their strengths, interests, and areas for development. This introspective practice involves reflecting on one's abilities, preferences, and values to gain insight into what drives and motivates them. A thorough self-assessment can guide career choices, personal development, and life decisions, leading to a more fulfilling and successful life. To effectively engage in self-assessment, it is important to explore various aspects such as skills, interests, values, personality traits, and experiences.

Skills are a fundamental component of self-assessment. These can be divided into hard skills and soft skills. Hard skills are technical abilities that are specific to a job or industry, such as coding, accounting, or graphic design. Soft skills, on the other hand, are interpersonal and transferable skills such as communication, teamwork, problem-solving, and leadership. Identifying your hard skills involves looking at your educational background, professional training, and work experience. Soft skills can be assessed by reflecting on how you interact with others, handle conflicts, and manage your time and tasks. Both types of skills are crucial in determining your strengths and should be considered in your self-assessment.

Interests are another vital element of self-assessment. Understanding what you enjoy doing can provide significant clues about suitable career paths and hobbies. To identify your interests, think about activities that make you lose track of time, topics you enjoy learning about, and tasks you look forward to. Consider your hobbies, pastimes, and the subjects that fascinated you during your education. Interests can also be assessed through career interest inventories, which are tools designed to match your preferences with potential careers. By exploring your interests, you can identify areas where you are likely to be motivated and engaged, leading to greater job satisfaction and personal fulfillment.

Values play a crucial role in self-assessment as they reflect what is important to you in life and work. Values influence your decision-making, behavior, and satisfaction with various aspects of life. Some common values include financial security, work-life balance, helping others, creativity, autonomy, and recognition. To identify your values, consider what you prioritize in your personal and professional life. Think about times when you felt fulfilled or, conversely, when you felt conflicted or dissatisfied. Values can be assessed through reflection, discussions with mentors or peers, and values clarification exercises. Understanding your values helps ensure that your career and life choices align with what truly matters to you, leading to a more meaningful and coherent life.

Personality traits are inherent characteristics that influence how you think, feel, and behave. Various personality assessments, such as the Myers-Briggs Type Indicator (MBTI), the Big Five personality traits, and the DISC assessment, can provide insights into your personality. For instance, the MBTI categorizes individuals into 16 personality types based on preferences in four dimensions: extraversion/ introversion, sensing/intuition, thinking/feeling, and judging/ perceiving. The Big Five assesses five broad dimensions: openness, conscientiousness, extraversion, agreeableness, and neuroticism. Understanding your personality traits can help you identify environments and roles where you are likely to thrive. For example, an introverted person may prefer solitary work or small team settings, while an extroverted person may excel in collaborative and dynamic environments.

Experiences, both personal and professional, are a rich source of information for self-assessment. Reflecting on your past experiences can help you identify patterns, strengths, and areas for growth. Consider your achievements, challenges, and the feedback you have received from others. What tasks or projects have you excelled in? What skills did you use or develop? How did you handle difficulties? Reflecting on these questions can provide valuable insights into your capabilities and preferences. Additionally, seeking feedback from colleagues, mentors, and friends can offer an external perspective on your strengths and areas for improvement.

Incorporating self-assessment tools and resources can enhance the process. Numerous online assessments and career exploration tools are available to help you systematically evaluate your skills, interests, values, and personality traits. Tools like the Strong Interest Inventory, the Career Anchors assessment, and various skill assessment tests can provide structured insights and guide your reflection. Career counseling and coaching are also valuable resources, offering professional guidance and support in interpreting assessment results and applying them to your career planning and personal development.

Self-assessment is not a one-time activity but an ongoing process. As you gain new experiences, acquire new skills, and your interests and values evolve, it is important to regularly reassess yourself. Periodic self-assessment allows you to stay aligned with your goals and make informed decisions that reflect your current state. Setting aside time for regular reflection, such as annual reviews or quarterly check-ins, can help you stay on track and adapt to changes in your life and career.

The benefits of self-assessment are numerous. It fosters self-awareness, which is the foundation for personal growth and effective decision-making. By understanding your strengths, you can build on them and seek opportunities that leverage your capabilities. Recognizing your interests can lead you to pursue passions that bring joy and fulfillment. Knowing your values ensures that your choices align with what is most important to you, enhancing your overall satisfaction and coherence in life. Understanding your personality traits helps you find environments and roles that suit your natural preferences, reducing stress and increasing your chances of success.

Moreover, self-assessment can enhance your career development. It enables you to identify suitable career paths, set realistic and meaningful goals, and create actionable plans to achieve them. By understanding your skills and areas for development, you can pursue targeted learning and development opportunities to enhance your competencies. Self-assessment also prepares you for job searches and interviews by helping you articulate your strengths and experiences clearly and confidently.

Chapter 3: The Value of Introverted Traits in the Workplace

In the contemporary workplace, introverted traits are often undervalued in favor of more extroverted qualities such as assertiveness, sociability, and charisma. However, introverts possess a unique set of characteristics and strengths that can significantly contribute to a successful and balanced work environment. Understanding the value of introverted traits involves exploring their impact on various aspects of work, including leadership, team dynamics, creativity, problem-solving, and overall workplace culture.

One of the most notable introverted traits is the ability to listen deeply and attentively. Introverts tend to be excellent listeners, often absorbing and processing information before responding. This trait can lead to more thoughtful and comprehensive decision-making, as introverts consider various perspectives and details. In a team setting, this quality fosters a culture of respect and inclusivity, as everyone feels heard and valued. Introverted leaders, in particular, can leverage this trait to build strong relationships with their team members, understand their concerns, and provide meaningful support and guidance.

Introverts are also known for their capacity for deep focus and concentration. They often prefer solitary work environments where they can immerse themselves in tasks without constant interruptions. This ability to concentrate deeply allows introverts to produce high-quality work, especially in roles that require detailed analysis, research, and complex problem-solving. In fields such as software development, writing, and scientific research, the introvert's propensity for focused, independent work is particularly advantageous. Their meticulous attention to detail can lead to fewer errors and more innovative solutions.

Creativity and innovation are other areas where introverted traits shine. Introverts often have rich inner lives and spend a significant amount of time reflecting and contemplating ideas. This introspective nature can lead to unique and creative approaches to challenges. Many renowned artists, writers, and scientists are introverts who have made groundbreaking contributions through their solitary work and deep thinking. In the workplace, encouraging introverts to explore and develop their ideas can lead to innovative products, services, and processes that drive organizational success.

In addition to their creative strengths, introverts tend to excel in strategic thinking and planning. Their preference for reflection and careful consideration means they are often adept at developing long-term strategies and anticipating potential challenges. Introverts are likely to weigh the pros and cons of various options, consider the broader context, and make well-informed decisions. This strategic approach is invaluable in roles that require planning, such as project management, financial analysis, and executive leadership. By carefully analyzing data and trends, introverts can guide organizations toward sustainable growth and stability.

Introverted leaders bring a unique and valuable perspective to management. Contrary to the common misconception that effective leaders must be extroverted, introverted leaders can be highly successful. They often lead by example, demonstrating integrity, humility, and a strong work ethic. Introverted leaders are typically more inclined to empower their team members, providing them with autonomy and opportunities to develop their skills. This leadership style can foster a sense of ownership and motivation among employees, leading to higher engagement and productivity. Furthermore, introverted leaders' emphasis on listening and understanding can create a supportive and collaborative team environment.

The ability to build deep and meaningful relationships is another key strength of introverts. While they may not seek out large social gatherings, introverts often excel in one-on-one interactions and small group settings. They are likely to form strong, trusting relationships with colleagues, clients, and stakeholders. This capacity for building genuine connections can be particularly valuable in roles that require long-term relationship management, such as client services, counseling, and human resources. Introverts' empathetic nature and attentiveness can make others feel valued and understood, fostering loyalty and trust.

In addition to their interpersonal strengths, introverts are often highly self-aware and reflective. They tend to be in tune with their own emotions and thoughts, which can lead to greater emotional intelligence. This self-awareness enables introverts to manage their emotions effectively, remain calm under pressure, and navigate complex social dynamics. In the workplace, emotional intelligence is crucial for effective communication, conflict resolution, and leadership. Introverts' ability to understand and manage their own emotions, as well as empathize with others, contributes to a positive and harmonious work environment.

The preference for preparation and thoroughness is another valuable trait of introverts. They often take the time to prepare meticulously for meetings, presentations, and projects. This attention to detail and commitment to excellence can lead to high-quality work and well-considered contributions. In roles that require precision and reliability, such as engineering, accounting, and quality assurance, the introvert's dedication to thoroughness is particularly beneficial. Their methodical approach ensures that tasks are completed accurately and efficiently, reducing the likelihood of errors and enhancing overall performance.

Introverts also tend to be adept at handling complex and challenging situations. Their calm and composed demeanor can be a stabilizing force in high-stress environments. Introverts are often able to think clearly and make rational decisions even under pressure. This ability to remain level-headed and focused is valuable in crisis management, emergency response, and other high-stakes roles. By approaching problems with a thoughtful and measured mindset, introverts can lead teams through difficult times and find effective solutions to pressing issues.

In terms of workplace culture, introverts contribute to creating a balanced and inclusive environment. Their preference for quieter, more low-key interactions can complement the more dynamic and energetic nature of extroverts, leading to a diverse and well-rounded team dynamic. Organizations that recognize and value the contributions of both introverts and extroverts can foster a more inclusive and supportive culture. This diversity of thought and approach can enhance creativity, problem-solving, and overall organizational effectiveness.

Moreover, introverts' preference for independent work can lead to increased productivity and innovation. By providing introverts with the flexibility to work in environments that suit their preferences, such as quiet spaces or remote work options, organizations can tap into their full potential. Allowing introverts to work autonomously and at their own pace can result in higher quality work and greater job satisfaction. Flexible work arrangements that accommodate different working styles contribute to a more inclusive and productive workplace.

Finally, introverts' resilience and adaptability are significant assets in the workplace. While they may prefer routine and stability, introverts are often able to adapt to changing circumstances and new challenges. Their reflective nature allows them to process and respond to changes thoughtfully and strategically. In today's fast-paced and ever-evolving work environment, the ability to adapt and thrive in the face of change is crucial. Introverts' resilience and adaptability enable them to navigate transitions and contribute to organizational success.

Chapter 4: Remote Work

Remote work has become increasingly popular, especially with advancements in technology and the global shift in work dynamics brought about by the COVID-19 pandemic. For introverts, remote work offers a unique opportunity to thrive in an environment that aligns well with their preferences and strengths. Understanding how to make the most of remote work can significantly enhance productivity, job satisfaction, and overall well-being for introverts. To fully explore this topic, it is important to consider various aspects, including the benefits of remote work for introverts, strategies for creating an effective home office environment, managing communication and collaboration, maintaining work-life balance, and addressing potential challenges.

One of the primary benefits of remote work for introverts is the ability to work in a controlled and personalized environment. Introverts often prefer quiet, low-stimulation settings where they can focus deeply without the distractions commonly found in traditional office environments. Working from home allows introverts to design their workspace to suit their preferences, whether that means a quiet room with minimal interruptions, calming décor, or the flexibility to choose their working hours. This level of control can lead to increased concentration and productivity, as introverts can create an environment that maximizes their comfort and efficiency.

The flexibility offered by remote work is another significant advantage for introverts. Many remote jobs allow for flexible scheduling, enabling introverts to work during their most productive times, whether early in the morning or late at night. This flexibility can also reduce the stress associated with commuting and rigid office hours, allowing introverts to manage their energy levels more effectively. By structuring their day in a way that aligns with their natural rhythms, introverts can optimize their performance and maintain a healthier work-life balance.

Remote work also minimizes the frequency and intensity of social interactions, which can be particularly beneficial for introverts. In a traditional office setting, introverts may find it draining to navigate constant meetings, impromptu discussions, and open-plan offices. Remote work allows for more deliberate and scheduled interactions, giving introverts the space to prepare and engage on their terms. Virtual meetings, emails, and instant messaging offer more control over the timing and nature of communication, reducing the social fatigue that can come with in-person interactions.

Creating an effective home office environment is crucial for thriving in remote work. Introverts should consider several factors when setting up their workspace. First, choosing a quiet and comfortable location is essential. This might be a dedicated room or a specific area in the home that minimizes noise and distractions. Investing in ergonomic furniture, such as a comfortable chair and an adjustable desk, can enhance physical comfort and reduce the risk of strain or injury.

Lighting and temperature are also important considerations. Natural light can improve mood and productivity, so positioning the workspace near a window can be beneficial. However, it's also important to have adjustable lighting for different times of the day. Maintaining a comfortable temperature and good air quality can further enhance the work environment. Plants can improve air quality and add a touch of nature to the workspace, contributing to a more pleasant and calming atmosphere.

Technology plays a critical role in remote work, and having the right tools is essential for success. A reliable computer, high-speed internet connection, and necessary software and applications are foundational. Introverts should also consider investing in noise-canceling headphones to block out external noise and create a focused work environment. Additionally, organizing digital files and using project management tools can help streamline workflows and reduce stress.

Managing communication and collaboration effectively is another key aspect of thriving in a remote work environment. While introverts may prefer fewer interactions, effective communication is still crucial for remote work success. Setting clear boundaries and expectations with colleagues and supervisors can help manage communication more effectively. This might include specifying preferred communication channels, such as email or instant messaging, and establishing regular check-ins to stay connected and informed.

Introverts can leverage their strength in written communication by crafting clear, concise, and thoughtful emails and messages. This not only reduces the need for frequent meetings but also ensures that communication is effective and efficient. When virtual meetings are necessary, introverts can prepare in advance by reviewing agendas, gathering necessary information, and formulating their thoughts. This preparation can boost confidence and contribute to more productive discussions.

Maintaining work-life balance is crucial for overall well-being, especially in a remote work setting where the boundaries between work and personal life can blur. Introverts should establish a clear routine that includes designated work hours and regular breaks. Creating a physical separation between work and living spaces, such as using a specific room or area for work, can help reinforce these boundaries. It is also important to set limits on work-related communications outside of designated work hours to ensure adequate time for rest and personal activities.

Incorporating regular breaks and time for self-care into the daily routine is essential. Introverts can benefit from activities that help them recharge and relax, such as reading, walking, meditating, or pursuing hobbies. Taking time to disconnect from work and engage in activities that bring joy and relaxation can prevent burnout and maintain mental and emotional health.

While remote work offers many benefits, it also presents potential challenges that introverts need to address. One common challenge is the feeling of isolation. Working from home can reduce opportunities for social interaction, leading to loneliness and disconnection. Introverts can mitigate this by scheduling regular virtual coffee chats or catch-ups with colleagues, participating in online communities or professional groups, and seeking social interactions outside of work.

Another challenge is maintaining visibility and recognition in a remote work environment. Introverts may need to make a conscious effort to showcase their work and contributions. This can be achieved by regularly updating supervisors and team members on progress, sharing achievements and milestones, and participating in team meetings and discussions. Seeking feedback and actively engaging in professional development opportunities can also enhance visibility and demonstrate commitment to growth and improvement.

Time management and self-discipline are critical for remote work success. Without the structure of a traditional office, introverts must manage their time effectively to meet deadlines and achieve goals. Setting specific, achievable daily and weekly goals can provide direction and motivation. Using productivity tools, such as to-do lists, calendars, and time-tracking apps, can help introverts stay organized and focused.

It is also important for introverts to advocate for their needs and preferences. This might involve discussing flexible working arrangements with supervisors, requesting adjustments to meeting schedules, or seeking support for managing workload. Open and honest communication about what helps them thrive can lead to a more supportive and accommodating work environment.

Chapter 5: Writing and Editing

Writing and editing as a career can be particularly well-suited to introverts, offering a unique opportunity to craft words and ideas in solitude. These fields allow individuals to leverage their introspective nature, attention to detail, and preference for quiet, focused work. Whether working as a freelance writer, an editor for a publishing house, or a content creator for various media platforms, writing and editing provide a fulfilling and flexible career path that aligns well with introverted traits. This comprehensive exploration will cover the advantages of writing and editing for introverts, the different career paths available, skills required, strategies for success, the importance of self-care, and the evolving landscape of the industry.

One of the primary advantages of writing and editing for introverts is the nature of the work itself. These professions typically involve spending long periods alone, working independently to develop content, refine ideas, and polish text. This solitude allows introverts to concentrate deeply without the interruptions and social demands that can be exhausting in more extroverted professions. The ability to work quietly and methodically is a significant asset in writing and editing, as these tasks often require meticulous attention to detail and the capacity to think critically and creatively.

The introspective nature of introverts is particularly beneficial in writing and editing. Writers and editors often need to reflect deeply on their subjects, characters, and narratives to produce compelling and coherent content. This reflection can lead to more thoughtful and nuanced work, as introverts are likely to consider multiple perspectives and delve into the complexities of their topics. Whether crafting fiction, non-fiction, technical documents, or marketing materials, the ability to engage deeply with the content is a key strength that introverts bring to the table.

Various career paths in writing and editing offer opportunities for introverts to find niches that suit their interests and skills. Freelance writing is a popular option, providing flexibility and autonomy. Freelance writers can work on diverse projects, from articles and blog posts to ghostwriting books and creating marketing content. This variety allows introverts to explore different subjects and styles, continually developing their skills and expertise.

In addition to freelance writing, technical writing is another promising career path. Technical writers create manuals, guides, and documentation for products and services, often requiring a deep understanding of complex information and the ability to communicate it clearly and concisely. This role is ideal for introverts who enjoy learning about new technologies and systems and who excel at breaking down complicated concepts into understandable content.

Editing offers a range of career options as well. Copyediting involves checking text for grammar, spelling, punctuation, and consistency, ensuring that the final product is polished and error-free. Substantive editing, also known as developmental editing, involves working more closely with the content and structure of a document, helping to shape the narrative, improve clarity, and enhance the overall quality of the writing. Both types of editing require a keen eye for detail and a deep understanding of language, skills that introverts often possess in abundance.

Skills required for success in writing and editing include strong language proficiency, attention to detail, creativity, and critical thinking. Writers need to be adept at constructing clear and engaging sentences, developing compelling narratives, and adapting their style to different audiences and purposes. Editors must have a thorough understanding of grammar and style, as well as the ability to identify and resolve issues in the text, from minor typographical errors to significant structural problems.

For both writers and editors, the ability to conduct thorough research is essential. This skill is particularly important for non-fiction writing, technical writing, and any content that requires factual accuracy and depth. Introverts' propensity for deep focus and independent work makes them well-suited to research-intensive tasks, as they can spend long periods gathering information, analyzing sources, and synthesizing data to create accurate and informative content.

Successful writers and editors also need to develop strong organizational and time management skills. Freelancers, in particular, must juggle multiple projects, meet deadlines, and manage their schedules effectively. Using tools such as project management software, calendars, and to-do lists can help introverts stay organized and ensure that they meet their commitments.

Networking and self-promotion, while sometimes challenging for introverts, are also important aspects of building a successful career in writing and editing. Building a professional network can lead to new opportunities, collaborations, and valuable feedback. Introverts can leverage their strengths in thoughtful communication and relationship-building by engaging in online communities, participating in writing groups or forums, and attending virtual workshops and conferences. Creating a strong online presence through a personal website, blog, or social media can also help writers and editors showcase their work and connect with potential clients or employers.

Self-care is crucial for sustaining a long-term career in writing and editing. The solitary nature of the work, while beneficial in many ways, can also lead to feelings of isolation and burnout if not managed carefully. Introverts should prioritize regular breaks, physical activity, and social interactions to maintain their mental and physical health. Setting boundaries between work and personal life, such as designating specific work hours and creating a dedicated workspace, can help maintain a healthy balance and prevent work from encroaching on personal time.

The landscape of writing and editing is continually evolving, presenting both challenges and opportunities. The rise of digital media has increased the demand for content, with writers and editors needed for websites, blogs, social media, and online publications. This shift has created new avenues for introverts to share their work and reach wider audiences. However, it also requires staying current with digital trends, SEO practices, and multimedia content creation.

The publishing industry is another area experiencing significant change. Traditional publishing houses are adapting to the digital age, while self-publishing has become a viable option for many writers. Self-publishing allows writers to retain more control over their work and reach audiences directly, though it also requires handling the responsibilities of marketing, distribution, and sales. Introverts interested in self-publishing can benefit from resources such as online courses, writing communities, and professional services to navigate the process and promote their books effectively.

Chapter 6: Graphic Design

Graphic design stands out as an exemplary career choice for introverts due to its inherent demand for visual creativity, which can be effectively nurtured in quiet, solitary spaces. This profession involves creating visual content to communicate messages, combining art and technology to produce a wide array of design elements including advertisements, websites, logos, brochures, and more. The very nature of graphic design aligns well with the strengths and preferences of introverts, making it an ideal career path for those who thrive in environments that offer both solitude and creative freedom.

Introverts often excel in environments where they can work independently or in small, focused groups, and graphic design provides ample opportunities for this. Many graphic designers work as freelancers or in small design studios, allowing them to have control over their work environment and schedule. This autonomy is crucial for introverts, as it enables them to manage their energy levels and productivity effectively. Working from home or in a quiet studio, introverts can immerse themselves in their creative process without the constant interruptions and social demands that are common in more extroverted professions.

The process of graphic design itself is highly introspective, involving a significant amount of solitary work. It begins with understanding the client's needs and objectives, which requires a deep level of thought and analysis—a strength of many introverts. Designers then move on to the conceptualization phase, where they brainstorm and develop ideas. This stage is typically done in isolation, allowing designers to tap into their inner creativity without external distractions. Introverts, who often have a rich inner world and a strong capacity for deep thinking, can thrive in this aspect of the job.

Once ideas are formulated, graphic designers use various tools and software to bring their visions to life. Mastery of these tools requires a blend of technical skill and creative intuition, a combination that introverts often excel at due to their preference for focused, detailed-oriented work. Software like Adobe Creative Suite (including Photoshop, Illustrator, and InDesign) demands a high level of concentration and precision, skills that introverts naturally possess. The iterative process of designing, receiving feedback, and refining the work is a cycle that allows for thoughtful reflection and gradual improvement, resonating well with the introverted disposition.

Moreover, graphic design is fundamentally about communication through visual means, reducing the necessity for constant verbal interaction. While communication with clients and team members is essential, much of it can be done through emails, written briefs, and visual drafts, allowing introverts to communicate effectively without extensive face-to-face meetings. This written form of communication often suits introverts better, as it gives them time to formulate their thoughts and respond thoughtfully, rather than having to think on their feet in spontaneous conversations.

In the modern digital age, the demand for graphic design skills is expanding rapidly. Virtually every industry requires graphic designers to create compelling visuals for their online presence, marketing materials, and branding efforts. This widespread demand means that introverts can find employment opportunities across various sectors, from tech companies to non-profits, each offering different working environments and levels of social interaction. The versatility of graphic design skills also allows introverts to explore niche markets or specialized fields that align with their personal interests, further enhancing job satisfaction and career fulfillment.

Freelancing in graphic design offers another layer of introvert-friendly benefits. Freelance graphic designers can choose their clients, projects, and work hours, providing an unparalleled level of flexibility. This career path enables introverts to create a work-life balance that suits their preferences, avoiding the burnout that can come from traditional 9-to-5 jobs. Additionally, the freelance model allows for periods of intense creative work followed by downtime, aligning well with the natural ebb and flow of an introvert's energy levels.

The collaborative aspects of graphic design, while sometimes challenging for introverts, can also be managed in ways that are conducive to their working style. Collaborations often occur over digital platforms, allowing introverts to contribute their ideas and feedback in a controlled manner. This digital collaboration reduces the need for in-person meetings, which can be draining for introverts, and allows them to engage at their own pace.

Furthermore, the field of graphic design is constantly evolving with new trends, tools, and technologies, providing continuous learning opportunities. Introverts, who often enjoy diving deep into subjects of interest, can find this aspect of the job particularly rewarding. Staying updated with the latest design trends and software advancements not only enhances their skills but also keeps the work exciting and engaging.

Chapter 7: Software Development

Software development is a prime career choice for introverts, offering an environment where they can leverage their analytical skills and deep focus to build innovative solutions. This profession involves designing, coding, testing, and maintaining software applications and systems, requiring a combination of technical knowledge, problem-solving abilities, and creativity. The field of software development aligns perfectly with the strengths and preferences of introverts, making it an ideal career path for those who excel in solitary, focused work environments.

At its core, software development is a task-oriented and project-based profession. Introverts often thrive in roles where they can work independently or in small, tight-knit teams. In software development, much of the work is done individually, with developers spending significant time writing and debugging code, designing system architectures, and implementing algorithms. This solo aspect of the job allows introverts to immerse themselves deeply in their tasks without the constant need for social interaction, enabling them to produce high-quality, well-thought-out work.

The process of software development begins with understanding user requirements and defining the scope of the project. This initial phase often involves detailed discussions with stakeholders to gather information and set objectives. While this may require some interaction, it is generally structured and purposeful, allowing introverts to prepare and contribute meaningfully. Once the requirements are clear, developers can retreat into the more solitary phases of the development cycle.

One of the most attractive aspects of software development for introverts is the focus on deep work. Writing and optimizing code requires a high level of concentration and attention to detail, both of which are areas where introverts excel. The ability to work uninterrupted for extended periods is crucial in this profession, as it allows developers to solve complex problems and create robust solutions. Introverts' natural inclination towards introspection and deep thinking makes them well-suited for this type of work.

Additionally, the iterative nature of software development—where developers write code, test it, and then refine it based on feedback—aligns well with introverted tendencies. This cycle allows for periods of intense focus followed by moments of reflection and analysis, giving introverts the opportunity to work at their own pace. The feedback process, often conducted through code reviews and testing, is typically structured and can be done asynchronously, reducing the need for constant real-time interactions.

The tools and technologies used in software development further enhance its suitability for introverts. Development environments, version control systems, and collaboration platforms are designed to facilitate individual productivity while enabling team communication. Tools like Git for version control, integrated development environments (IDEs) like Visual Studio Code or IntelliJ IDEA, and project management platforms like Jira or Trello help developers organize their work, track progress, and collaborate efficiently without the need for frequent meetings. This setup allows introverts to communicate effectively in writing, a mode of communication they often find more comfortable and less draining than verbal exchanges.

Remote work is another significant advantage of a career in software development, offering introverts the ability to work from home or other quiet environments where they can control their surroundings. The tech industry has long been a pioneer in remote work practices, and many companies offer flexible work arrangements. This flexibility not only allows introverts to create a work environment that minimizes distractions and overstimulation but also enables them to manage their energy levels and maintain a healthy work-life balance. The rise of remote work has also expanded job opportunities, allowing introverts to find roles that match their skills and interests without being limited by geographic location.

Moreover, the collaborative aspect of software development, while essential, is often managed in ways that accommodate introverted working styles. Teams frequently use asynchronous communication methods, such as emails, messaging apps like Slack, and collaboration tools like GitHub, to discuss projects and share updates. This approach allows introverts to participate fully without the pressure of real-time conversations. When meetings are necessary, they are often well-structured with clear agendas, enabling introverts to prepare in advance and contribute thoughtfully.

The demand for software developers is robust and growing, with virtually every industry seeking to harness the power of technology to improve efficiency, create new products, and stay competitive. This high demand translates into a wide array of job opportunities, from developing consumer apps and enterprise software to working on cutting-edge technologies like artificial intelligence, machine learning, and blockchain. Introverts can find roles that align with their specific interests and strengths, whether it's front-end development, back-end development, full-stack development, data science, or cybersecurity.

Continuous learning is a hallmark of the software development field, as new languages, frameworks, and tools are constantly emerging. Introverts, who often enjoy deep dives into subjects of interest, can find this aspect of the job particularly rewarding. The need to stay updated with the latest trends and advancements not only enhances their skills but also keeps the work intellectually stimulating and engaging. Online courses, coding bootcamps, and developer communities provide ample opportunities for introverts to learn and grow at their own pace, often from the comfort of their own space.

Chapter 8: Data Analysis

Data analysis is an exceptionally fitting career for introverts, offering a blend of independent work, deep thinking, and a structured approach to problem-solving. This profession involves examining data sets to extract meaningful insights, trends, and patterns, which are then used to inform decision-making processes across various industries. Data analysts utilize statistical tools, programming languages, and data visualization techniques to transform raw data into valuable information. The nature of data analysis aligns well with the strengths and preferences of introverts, making it an ideal career path for those who thrive in environments that prioritize focus, precision, and intellectual rigor.

One of the primary reasons data analysis is well-suited for introverts is the emphasis on solitary work. Data analysts spend significant amounts of time working independently, poring over data sets, cleaning and organizing data, and conducting statistical analyses. This solitary aspect allows introverts to immerse themselves in their tasks without the constant need for social interaction, enabling them to concentrate deeply and produce high-quality work. The meticulous and detail-oriented nature of data analysis appeals to introverts who excel at tasks requiring sustained attention and careful examination.

The process of data analysis begins with data collection and cleaning, which involves gathering data from various sources and ensuring its accuracy and consistency. This stage is crucial, as the quality of the data directly impacts the reliability of the analysis. Introverts often find satisfaction in the methodical and systematic approach required for data cleaning, as it allows them to engage in focused, repetitive tasks that require precision and attention to detail. The solitude of this phase provides introverts with the quiet time they need to think critically and work methodically.

Once the data is prepared, data analysts move on to the exploration and analysis phase, where they apply statistical techniques to uncover patterns and trends. This stage involves using software tools like Excel, R, Python, and SQL to manipulate data and perform complex calculations. Introverts' natural affinity for analytical thinking and problem-solving shines in this aspect of the job. They can delve deeply into the data, exploring different angles and hypotheses, and derive insights that might not be immediately apparent. The ability to work independently and focus intensely on these tasks allows introverts to excel and produce insightful, accurate analyses.

Data visualization is another key component of data analysis, involving the creation of charts, graphs, and dashboards to present findings in a clear and compelling manner. Tools like Tableau, Power BI, and matplotlib are commonly used for this purpose. Introverts often have a keen eye for detail and aesthetics, which helps them design effective visualizations that communicate complex information succinctly. The process of creating visualizations is typically a solitary activity that allows introverts to concentrate fully on the task at hand, ensuring that the final product is both informative and visually appealing.

The communication aspect of data analysis, while essential, is often structured and can be managed in ways that suit introverts' preferences. Presenting findings to stakeholders or team members is a crucial part of the job, but much of this communication can be done through written reports, emails, or pre-recorded presentations. This allows introverts to prepare thoroughly and convey their insights in a clear, thoughtful manner, without the pressure of spontaneous verbal communication. When face-to-face meetings or presentations are necessary, the structured nature of these interactions helps introverts feel more comfortable and confident, as they can plan and rehearse their points in advance.

The demand for data analysts spans across various industries, including finance, healthcare, marketing, technology, and government. This wide range of applications means that introverts can find roles that align with their interests and strengths, whether it's analyzing financial trends, studying patient outcomes, or optimizing marketing strategies. The versatility of data analysis skills also allows introverts to explore different fields and industries, providing a dynamic and varied career path.

Remote work is another significant advantage of a career in data analysis. The tech industry has embraced remote work, and many companies offer flexible arrangements that allow data analysts to work from home or other quiet environments. This flexibility is particularly beneficial for introverts, as it enables them to create a work environment that minimizes distractions and overstimulation, fostering productivity and well-being. The ability to work remotely also opens up more job opportunities, as introverts are not limited by geographic location and can find roles that best match their skills and interests.

Furthermore, the collaborative aspects of data analysis can be managed in ways that accommodate introverted working styles. Teams often use asynchronous communication methods, such as emails, messaging apps, and collaboration tools, to discuss projects and share updates. This approach allows introverts to participate fully without the pressure of real-time conversations. When meetings are necessary, they are typically well-structured with clear agendas, enabling introverts to prepare in advance and contribute thoughtfully.

The field of data analysis is continually evolving, with new tools, techniques, and methodologies emerging regularly. This constant evolution provides continuous learning opportunities, which can be particularly appealing to introverts who enjoy deep dives into subjects of interest. Staying updated with the latest trends and advancements not only enhances their skills but also keeps the work intellectually stimulating and engaging. Online courses, webinars, and professional communities offer ample opportunities for introverts to learn and grow at their own pace, often from the comfort of their own space.

In addition to technical skills, successful data analysts often possess strong critical thinking and problem-solving abilities. Introverts' natural inclination towards introspection and deep thinking makes them well-suited for these aspects of the job. They can approach complex problems methodically, considering various factors and potential solutions before making decisions. This thoughtful and deliberate approach helps ensure that their analyses are thorough and well-reasoned, leading to more accurate and reliable insights.

Chapter 9: Librarianship

Librarianship is a quintessentially introvert-friendly career, offering an environment where individuals can immerse themselves in the world of knowledge and information while working in a tranquil and structured setting. Librarians play a vital role in managing and organizing library resources, assisting patrons with research, and fostering a love of reading and learning within their communities. The profession encompasses a variety of roles, including public librarians, academic librarians, school librarians, and special librarians, each with its own unique focus and responsibilities. The nature of librarianship aligns well with the strengths and preferences of introverts, making it an ideal career path for those who excel in quiet, reflective, and intellectually stimulating environments.

One of the primary reasons librarianship is well-suited for introverts is the emphasis on independent work and attention to detail. Librarians are responsible for cataloging and classifying library materials, maintaining accurate records, and managing collections. These tasks require a high level of concentration and meticulousness, qualities that many introverts naturally possess. The solitary nature of these activities allows introverts to work quietly and methodically, ensuring that library resources are well-organized and easily accessible to patrons.

In addition to cataloging, librarians engage in research and information retrieval, assisting patrons in finding the information they need. This aspect of the job often involves in-depth searches of databases, reference materials, and digital resources. Introverts, who typically enjoy delving deeply into subjects of interest, can thrive in this role, using their analytical skills and intellectual curiosity to uncover valuable information. The process of conducting research is usually a solitary activity that allows introverts to focus deeply and work at their own pace.

Librarians also play a crucial role in information literacy education, teaching patrons how to effectively find, evaluate, and use information. This educational aspect can involve one-on-one instruction, workshops, and the creation of online guides and tutorials. While this may require some interaction with patrons, it is often structured and purposeful, allowing introverts to prepare and present information in a thoughtful and organized manner. The ability to educate others about information literacy is deeply rewarding for many introverts, who find satisfaction in helping others develop their skills and knowledge.

Moreover, librarianship offers ample opportunities for introverts to engage in meaningful behind-the-scenes work. Collection development, for example, involves selecting and acquiring new materials for the library based on community needs and interests. This process requires careful consideration, research, and collaboration with other library staff, but much of the work can be done independently. Introverts can take pleasure in curating a diverse and relevant collection that enriches the library's offerings and serves the needs of its patrons.

Library programming and events are another important aspect of librarianship, providing opportunities for community engagement and outreach. While organizing events may seem extroverted, many aspects of the planning process, such as brainstorming ideas, coordinating logistics, and creating promotional materials, are tasks that introverts can handle independently. Additionally, libraries often host a wide range of programs, from book clubs and author talks to quiet activities like crafting workshops and film screenings, allowing introverts to choose involvement in events that align with their comfort levels and interests.

The rise of digital librarianship has further expanded the role of librarians, incorporating responsibilities related to managing digital resources, maintaining library websites, and creating online content. Digital librarians work with e-books, online databases, and digital archives, ensuring that these resources are accessible and user-friendly.

This digital focus provides even more opportunities for introverts to work in quiet, tech-focused environments, utilizing their skills in information technology and digital management. The shift towards digital libraries also allows for remote work options, enabling introverts to work from home or other quiet spaces where they can concentrate fully on their tasks.

Academic librarianship, in particular, offers a research-intensive environment that can be highly appealing to introverts. Academic librarians support the research needs of students, faculty, and researchers at colleges and universities. They provide specialized reference services, develop research guides, and offer instruction on information literacy and research methodologies. This role often involves collaboration with academic departments and participation in scholarly activities, but much of the work is conducted independently, allowing introverts to delve deeply into research topics and develop expertise in specific subject areas.

School librarians, also known as media specialists, play a critical role in supporting the educational goals of K-12 schools. They manage school library collections, assist with curriculum development, and promote literacy and a love of reading among students. School librarians often work closely with teachers to integrate library resources into classroom instruction, providing support for research projects and fostering information literacy skills. While school librarians interact with students and staff, the interactions are generally structured and purposeful, allowing introverts to build meaningful connections without overwhelming social demands.

Special librarians work in specialized settings such as law firms, medical institutions, corporations, and government agencies. They manage specialized collections and provide targeted information services to support the specific needs of their organizations. Special librarians often develop deep expertise in their fields, conducting detailed research and staying abreast of the latest developments and trends. This role requires a high level of specialized knowledge and analytical skills, making it an ideal fit for introverts who enjoy becoming subject matter experts and working in focused, niche areas.

The physical environment of libraries also contributes to their appeal for introverts. Libraries are typically quiet, orderly spaces designed to facilitate reading, study, and reflection. The serene atmosphere allows introverts to work comfortably and concentrate on their tasks without the distractions and noise often found in more extroverted work environments. Libraries also provide designated quiet areas and private workspaces, further enhancing the ability of introverts to focus and work independently.

Librarianship offers a balanced blend of routine tasks and intellectual challenges, providing a satisfying and varied work experience. The profession requires a combination of organizational skills, research abilities, and a passion for knowledge and information. Introverts, who often excel in these areas, can find a fulfilling career in librarianship that allows them to contribute meaningfully to their communities while working in an environment that aligns with their strengths and preferences.

Chapter 10: Freelancing

Freelancing offers a unique and appealing career path for many, particularly for introverts who often thrive in environments that allow for greater autonomy, flexibility, and control over their work. Building a career as a freelancer involves creating opportunities that align with personal strengths and preferences, providing a platform to harness one's skills and interests without the constraints of traditional employment structures. To explore this topic comprehensively, it is essential to delve into the benefits of freelancing for introverts, strategies for success, managing client relationships, maintaining work-life balance, navigating financial and logistical challenges, and leveraging personal branding and networking.

One of the most significant benefits of freelancing for introverts is the ability to work independently. Introverts often prefer solitary or low-stimulation environments where they can concentrate deeply without frequent interruptions. Freelancing allows them to create such an environment, tailored to their preferences and needs. This autonomy over one's workspace can lead to enhanced productivity and creativity, as introverts can design a setting that maximizes their comfort and efficiency. Whether working from a home office, a quiet café, or a co-working space, freelancers have the freedom to choose where and how they work best.

Flexibility is another critical advantage of freelancing. Introverts often benefit from flexible schedules that enable them to work during their most productive times. Freelancers can set their own hours, taking breaks as needed to recharge and manage their energy levels effectively. This flexibility can reduce the stress associated with rigid office hours and commuting, allowing introverts to balance work with personal activities and responsibilities more seamlessly. For instance, an introverted freelancer might prefer working in the early morning or late at night when distractions are minimal, leading to more focused and productive work sessions.

Freelancing also minimizes the need for constant social interactions, which can be draining for introverts. Traditional office environments often require frequent meetings, spontaneous discussions, and social events that can overwhelm introverted individuals. In contrast, freelancing enables introverts to control the frequency and nature of their interactions, engaging with clients and colleagues primarily through scheduled meetings, emails, and virtual communication tools. This controlled interaction allows introverts to prepare and engage more thoughtfully, reducing social fatigue and enhancing the quality of their professional relationships.

Building a successful freelance career involves several key strategies. First, identifying and honing one's core skills is essential. Freelancers should focus on areas where they excel and enjoy working, whether it is writing, graphic design, web development, consulting, or another field. Developing a niche expertise can help differentiate oneself in a competitive market and attract clients who value specialized skills. Continuous learning and professional development are crucial for staying current with industry trends and maintaining a competitive edge.

Creating a strong online presence is another vital strategy for freelance success. A professional website that showcases a freelancer's portfolio, services, testimonials, and contact information can serve as a central hub for attracting clients. Regularly updating the site with new work samples, blog posts, and client success stories can demonstrate expertise and credibility. Leveraging social media platforms and professional networks like LinkedIn can further enhance visibility and connect freelancers with potential clients and collaborators.

Effective communication and project management skills are essential for freelancers to manage client relationships successfully. Setting clear expectations from the outset regarding project scope, timelines, deliverables, and payment terms can prevent misunderstandings and ensure smooth collaborations. Regular updates and transparent communication throughout the project lifecycle help build trust and keep clients informed. Introverts' strength in written communication can be particularly advantageous here, allowing them to convey ideas and updates clearly and professionally.

Managing client relationships also involves negotiating terms and handling feedback. Freelancers should feel empowered to negotiate rates and project terms that reflect their value and expertise. This might involve discussing budgets, timelines, and specific requirements to ensure mutual agreement. Handling feedback constructively is crucial; introverts can use their reflective nature to consider client feedback thoughtfully, making necessary adjustments while maintaining their professional integrity and vision.

Maintaining work-life balance is another critical aspect of freelancing, especially given the potential for blurred boundaries between work and personal life. Introverts should establish a routine that includes designated work hours, regular breaks, and time for relaxation and self-care. Creating a physical separation between work and living spaces, such as a dedicated home office, can reinforce these boundaries and promote a healthier balance. Time management tools and techniques, such as to-do lists, calendars, and productivity apps, can help freelancers stay organized and on track.

Freelancing can present financial and logistical challenges that introverts need to navigate. Income variability is a common concern, as freelance work often involves fluctuating workloads and payment schedules. Building a financial cushion and budgeting carefully can help manage this uncertainty. Diversifying income streams by offering a range of services or working with multiple clients can also provide more stability. Freelancers should keep accurate records of income and expenses, consider working with an accountant, and stay informed about tax obligations and business regulations.

Personal branding and networking are crucial for growing a freelance career, even for introverts who may find traditional networking events daunting. Introverts can leverage their strengths in thoughtful communication and relationship-building to create a strong personal brand. This might involve sharing insights and expertise through blog posts, articles, podcasts, or online courses, positioning oneself as a thought leader in their field. Engaging with online communities, participating in industry forums, and attending virtual events can provide networking opportunities without the need for extensive in-person interactions.

Building and maintaining a professional network is essential for finding clients, collaborators, and mentors. Introverts can focus on quality over quantity, developing deeper connections with a smaller group of contacts. Following up with clients and peers after projects, seeking feedback, and staying in touch through occasional check-ins can help sustain these relationships. Joining professional associations or local business groups can also provide valuable networking opportunities and resources.

Another important aspect of freelancing is continuous self-improvement and resilience. The freelance market is dynamic, and staying adaptable is crucial for long-term success. Freelancers should seek feedback, reflect on their experiences, and be open to learning and evolving. This might involve taking courses to acquire new skills, experimenting with different types of projects, or exploring new markets. Building resilience involves developing a mindset that embraces challenges as opportunities for growth and learning.

Chapter 11: Research and Development

Research and development (R&D) is a highly suitable career path for introverts, offering an environment that emphasizes deep thinking, creativity, and innovation, often conducted in quiet, focused settings. R&D professionals work across various industries, including technology, pharmaceuticals, engineering, and consumer goods, to develop new products, improve existing ones, and advance scientific knowledge. The nature of R&D aligns well with the strengths and preferences of introverts, making it an ideal career for those who excel in independent work, critical thinking, and detailed analysis.

At its core, R&D involves the systematic investigation and experimentation aimed at discovering new knowledge and applying it to create innovative solutions. This process typically begins with identifying a problem or opportunity, followed by extensive research to understand the underlying principles and potential solutions. Introverts often thrive in this initial phase, as it requires deep concentration, analytical skills, and a methodical approach to gathering and interpreting data. The ability to work independently and focus intensely on complex problems allows introverts to excel in these activities, producing high-quality, insightful research.

Once the initial research is completed, R&D professionals move on to the experimentation and development phases. This involves designing and conducting experiments, analyzing results, and iterating on their designs based on the findings. Introverts' natural inclination towards introspection and detailed analysis makes them well-suited for this aspect of the job. They can delve deeply into the experimental process, meticulously recording observations, and refining their approaches to achieve the desired outcomes. The solitary nature of much of this work allows introverts to concentrate fully on their tasks without the distractions and interruptions common in more extroverted work environments.

Collaboration is an essential component of R&D, but it is often structured in a way that suits introverts' working styles. R&D teams frequently consist of small, focused groups of specialists who bring different expertise to the table. These teams work together to solve complex problems, but much of the collaboration is conducted through written reports, structured meetings, and asynchronous communication methods such as emails and collaborative software. This approach allows introverts to prepare their contributions thoughtfully and engage in meaningful discussions without the pressure of constant verbal interaction. When meetings are necessary, they are typically well-organized with clear agendas, enabling introverts to participate effectively and confidently.

The field of R&D also offers a high degree of autonomy and flexibility, which is particularly appealing to introverts. Many R&D professionals have the freedom to set their own research agendas, choose their projects, and determine the direction of their work. This autonomy allows introverts to manage their energy levels and work at their own pace, fostering a productive and satisfying work environment. Additionally, the ability to work on projects that align with their personal interests and passions enhances job satisfaction and motivation, providing a sense of purpose and fulfillment.

One of the most appealing aspects of a career in R&D for introverts is the opportunity to engage in continuous learning and intellectual growth. The nature of research involves staying abreast of the latest developments in one's field, reading scientific literature, and attending conferences and workshops. Introverts, who often enjoy diving deeply into subjects of interest, can find this aspect of the job particularly rewarding. The constant pursuit of new knowledge and the challenge of solving complex problems provide intellectual stimulation and keep the work engaging and dynamic.

R&D in the technology sector, for example, involves developing cutting-edge software, hardware, and digital solutions. This field requires a blend of creativity and technical expertise, making it ideal for introverts who enjoy working with technology and solving intricate problems. Software development, artificial intelligence, cybersecurity, and data science are just a few areas where R&D professionals can make significant contributions. The tech industry's embrace of remote work and flexible schedules further enhances its appeal for introverts, allowing them to work in environments that suit their preferences and maximize their productivity.

In the pharmaceutical and biotechnology industries, R&D professionals conduct research to develop new drugs, medical devices, and therapeutic approaches. This work involves extensive laboratory experimentation, data analysis, and regulatory compliance. Introverts who excel in scientific research and have a passion for improving human health can find fulfilling careers in this field. The meticulous nature of laboratory work, combined with the opportunity to make a meaningful impact on patient outcomes, provides a sense of purpose and accomplishment.

Engineering R&D encompasses a wide range of disciplines, including mechanical, electrical, chemical, and civil engineering. Engineers in R&D roles focus on developing new technologies, materials, and processes to address practical challenges and improve existing systems. Introverts with strong analytical and problem-solving skills can thrive in this field, working on projects that require deep technical knowledge and innovative thinking. The collaborative yet structured nature of engineering teams allows introverts to contribute their expertise while maintaining a comfortable level of interaction.

Consumer goods R&D involves developing new products and improving existing ones to meet consumer needs and preferences. This field requires a combination of market research, product design, and testing. Introverts who enjoy understanding consumer behavior and creating innovative solutions can find rewarding careers in this area. The ability to work behind the scenes, conducting research and experiments, aligns well with introverted strengths and provides a fulfilling way to contribute to the development of products that enhance people's lives.

R&D roles in academia and government agencies offer additional opportunities for introverts to engage in meaningful research. Academic researchers often work at universities and research institutions, conducting studies to advance scientific knowledge and publish their findings in scholarly journals. This environment provides a high degree of intellectual freedom and the opportunity to collaborate with other researchers while maintaining a focus on independent work. Government agencies also conduct research to inform public policy and address societal challenges, offering introverts the chance to contribute to the public good through their work.

The physical work environment in R&D settings is typically conducive to introverts' preferences. Laboratories, research facilities, and offices are often designed to minimize distractions and provide quiet spaces for focused work. Introverts can take advantage of these environments to immerse themselves in their research, free from the noise and interruptions that can hinder productivity. The availability of private workspaces and the ability to control their surroundings further enhance introverts' ability to concentrate and perform at their best.

Chapter 12: Therapy and Counseling

Therapy and counseling are deeply rewarding careers that can be particularly well-suited for introverts. These professions involve working closely with individuals to help them navigate personal challenges, mental health issues, and emotional difficulties. The one-on-one nature of therapy and counseling aligns well with the strengths and preferences of introverts, making these careers an ideal choice for those who excel in empathetic listening, thoughtful analysis, and deep, meaningful interactions.

At the heart of therapy and counseling is the therapeutic relationship, a unique and confidential connection between the therapist and the client. This relationship is built on trust, empathy, and understanding, qualities that many introverts naturally possess. Introverts are often excellent listeners, able to provide their undivided attention and create a safe, non-judgmental space for clients to express their thoughts and feelings. This ability to listen deeply and empathetically is crucial in therapy, as it allows clients to feel heard and validated, fostering a strong therapeutic alliance.

Therapists and counselors use a variety of techniques and approaches to help clients address their concerns. These can include cognitive-behavioral therapy (CBT), psychodynamic therapy, humanistic therapy, and other evidence-based practices. Introverts, who often excel in analytical and reflective thinking, can effectively apply these methods to explore the underlying issues affecting their clients. By carefully analyzing clients' narratives and behavioral patterns, therapists can develop tailored treatment plans that address specific needs and goals.

One significant advantage of a career in therapy and counseling for introverts is the structured and predictable nature of the work. Sessions are typically scheduled in advance, providing a clear framework for the day and allowing therapists to prepare thoroughly for each client.

This structure reduces the unpredictability and social overstimulation that can be challenging for introverts, enabling them to focus on their clients with calm and confidence. Additionally, the one-on-one setting of therapy sessions minimizes the need for large group interactions, which can be draining for introverts.

The process of becoming a therapist or counselor involves extensive education and training, including obtaining a relevant degree, completing supervised clinical hours, and obtaining licensure. This rigorous training process can be particularly appealing to introverts who enjoy academic pursuits and the deep dive into the study of human behavior and mental health. The path to becoming a therapist often includes coursework in psychology, counseling theories, ethics, and clinical practice, providing a comprehensive foundation for professional practice. Introverts can thrive in this educational environment, where they can engage in focused study and develop a thorough understanding of their field.

Specialization within therapy and counseling offers further opportunities for introverts to find their niche. For example, some therapists specialize in working with specific populations, such as children and adolescents, couples, families, or individuals with specific mental health disorders. Others may focus on particular therapeutic modalities, such as art therapy, music therapy, or mindfulness-based approaches. Introverts can choose a specialization that aligns with their interests and strengths, allowing them to work in areas where they feel most passionate and effective.

Private practice is a common career path for many therapists and counselors, offering a high degree of autonomy and control over one's work environment. Introverts who prefer to work independently can find great satisfaction in running their own practice, where they can set their own schedules, choose their clients, and create a calming and comfortable office space. Private practice allows therapists to work at their own pace, manage their caseloads, and ensure that they have sufficient time for self-care and professional development.

Another appealing aspect of therapy and counseling for introverts is the potential for remote or teletherapy services. Advances in technology have made it possible for therapists to conduct sessions via video conferencing, providing greater flexibility and convenience for both therapists and clients. Teletherapy allows introverts to work from the comfort of their own homes or other quiet environments, reducing the need for commuting and allowing for greater control over their work settings. This flexibility can enhance job satisfaction and work-life balance, making the profession even more attractive to introverts.

In addition to one-on-one therapy, counselors often engage in other activities that align with introverted strengths. These can include conducting assessments, writing case notes, developing treatment plans, and participating in continuing education. The analytical and reflective nature of these tasks allows introverts to work quietly and independently, utilizing their skills in critical thinking and detailed documentation. The balance between client-facing work and these behind-the-scenes activities provides a varied and fulfilling work experience.

Therapists and counselors also have the opportunity to engage in research and contribute to the advancement of the field. Those who are inclined towards academic pursuits can conduct studies, publish articles, and present their findings at conferences. This aspect of the profession allows introverts to delve deeply into topics of interest, contribute to the evidence base, and influence clinical practice. The combination of clinical work and research can provide a rich and intellectually stimulating career.

The impact of therapy and counseling on clients' lives can be profoundly rewarding. Helping individuals navigate their challenges, develop coping strategies, and achieve personal growth provides a deep sense of purpose and fulfillment. Introverts, who often seek meaningful and impactful work, can find great satisfaction in seeing their clients make progress and improve their well-being. The ability to make a tangible difference in others' lives is a powerful motivator and a source of ongoing professional gratification.

Moreover, the therapeutic profession emphasizes self-awareness and personal growth, both for clients and therapists. Therapists often engage in their own therapy, supervision, and self-reflection to ensure they provide the best possible care for their clients. This focus on self-care and professional development aligns well with introverts' introspective nature, encouraging them to continually grow and evolve both personally and professionally.

Chapter 13: Archivist

An archivist plays a crucial role in preserving history, particularly in the digital age, and this career can be especially appealing to introverts. The profession involves the collection, organization, management, and preservation of records and documents that have historical, cultural, or evidentiary significance. Archivists work in a variety of settings, including museums, libraries, government agencies, universities, corporations, and non-profit organizations. The meticulous and often solitary nature of archival work, combined with the opportunity to engage deeply with historical materials, makes it an ideal career choice for introverts who excel in detailed, reflective, and independent work environments.

The core responsibility of an archivist is to appraise, acquire, and preserve records and documents that are of enduring value. This process begins with identifying and evaluating materials that should be archived, which can include manuscripts, letters, photographs, maps, electronic records, and more. Introverts, who often possess strong analytical skills and attention to detail, are well-suited for this task. They can carefully assess the historical significance and authenticity of documents, ensuring that valuable records are preserved for future generations.

Once materials are acquired, archivists must organize and catalog them in a systematic manner. This involves creating detailed descriptions, inventories, and finding aids that facilitate access to the archives. Introverts, who thrive in structured and orderly environments, excel in this aspect of the job. They can meticulously arrange and describe collections, making them easily accessible to researchers, historians, and the general public. The process of cataloging and organizing archives requires patience, concentration, and a methodical approach, qualities that many introverts naturally possess.

In addition to physical documents, archivists increasingly deal with digital records in the digital age. Digital archiving presents unique challenges, such as ensuring the longevity of electronic records, managing large volumes of data, and maintaining the integrity and authenticity of digital files. Introverts with a strong aptitude for technology can excel in digital archiving, using their skills to implement digital preservation strategies, manage electronic records management systems (ERMS), and develop metadata standards. The ability to work quietly and independently on these complex tasks makes digital archiving an attractive field for introverts.

One significant aspect of archival work is ensuring the proper storage and conservation of materials. Archivists must be knowledgeable about preservation techniques to protect records from damage due to environmental factors, such as light, temperature, humidity, and pests. They may also need to perform conservation treatments, such as repairing torn documents or digitizing fragile items to reduce handling. Introverts, who often prefer hands-on, focused work, can find satisfaction in these preservation activities. The meticulous nature of conservation work, coupled with the opportunity to work in quiet, controlled environments, aligns well with introverted preferences.

Archivists also play a vital role in providing access to archival materials. This can involve assisting researchers, answering reference questions, and facilitating access to collections. While this aspect of the job requires interaction with the public, it is usually conducted in a structured and purposeful manner. Introverts, who may prefer one-on-one or small group interactions over large social settings, can thrive in these situations. They can provide thoughtful, informed assistance to researchers, drawing on their deep knowledge of the collections and their ability to listen carefully to patrons' needs.

The digital age has transformed the way archives are accessed and used, with many institutions making their collections available online.

Archivists are often responsible for managing digital repositories, creating online exhibits, and ensuring that digital collections are accessible to a global audience. This aspect of the job allows introverts to combine their interest in history with their technical skills, working behind the scenes to curate and maintain digital archives. The creation of digital exhibits and virtual archives also offers introverts the opportunity to engage in creative and intellectually stimulating projects that can reach a wide audience without the need for extensive face-to-face interaction.

In addition to managing physical and digital archives, archivists are often involved in outreach and public programming. This can include giving presentations, organizing exhibitions, conducting workshops, and collaborating with educators to incorporate archival materials into curricula. While these activities require public speaking and interaction, they are typically well-planned and allow introverts to prepare thoroughly in advance. The ability to share their passion for history and archival work in a structured and meaningful way can be highly rewarding for introverts, who may find satisfaction in educating others and promoting the importance of archival preservation.

Continuing education and professional development are important aspects of an archivist's career. The field of archival science is constantly evolving, with new technologies, methodologies, and best practices emerging regularly. Introverts, who often enjoy learning and intellectual growth, can find fulfillment in staying current with developments in the field. This can involve attending conferences, participating in workshops, joining professional organizations, and pursuing advanced certifications. The opportunity to engage in lifelong learning and deepen their expertise can be particularly appealing to introverts who value knowledge and professional excellence.

The work environment of an archivist is typically conducive to introverts' preferences. Archives are often quiet, controlled spaces designed to protect and preserve valuable materials. The nature of archival work allows for long periods of focused, independent activity, free from the constant interruptions and noise found in more extroverted work environments. The ability to work in a serene and orderly setting enhances introverts' productivity and job satisfaction, allowing them to immerse themselves in their work and achieve a high level of precision and accuracy.

Moreover, archivists often have the opportunity to work on unique and historically significant projects. This can include processing collections of famous individuals, preserving rare manuscripts, and curating exhibitions on important historical events. The chance to engage with rare and valuable materials, and to contribute to the preservation of cultural heritage, provides a deep sense of purpose and fulfillment. Introverts, who often seek meaningful and impactful work, can find great satisfaction in knowing that their efforts help safeguard history for future generations.

Chapter 14: Accountancy

Accountancy, often perceived as a meticulous and highly specialized field, offers a wealth of opportunities for introverts who thrive in environments that demand precision, analytical thinking, and attention to detail. This career revolves around the systematic recording, analyzing, and reporting of financial transactions, providing critical insights that help organizations and individuals make informed economic decisions. Accountancy's structured and detail-oriented nature, along with its demand for solitary, focused work, aligns well with the strengths and preferences of introverts, making it an ideal career choice for those who excel in methodical, independent, and reflective tasks.

At the core of accountancy is the preparation and maintenance of financial records. Accountants are responsible for ensuring the accuracy and completeness of financial data, which involves tasks such as bookkeeping, preparing financial statements, and reconciling accounts. Introverts, who often excel in tasks that require concentration and meticulous attention to detail, are well-suited for these responsibilities. The ability to work independently on complex financial data allows introverts to immerse themselves in their work, applying their analytical skills to ensure that every transaction is accurately recorded and accounted for.

One of the primary roles of accountants is to prepare and analyze financial statements, including balance sheets, income statements, and cash flow statements. These documents provide a comprehensive overview of an organization's financial health, enabling stakeholders to make informed decisions. Introverts, who often possess strong analytical and critical thinking skills, can effectively interpret these statements, identifying trends, patterns, and discrepancies. This analytical prowess is crucial for providing insights that can drive strategic decision-making and ensure the long-term financial stability of the organization.

In addition to financial statement preparation, accountants are involved in budgeting and forecasting. This process requires a deep understanding of the organization's financial history, current performance, and future goals. Introverts, who excel in detailed and methodical analysis, can create accurate and realistic budgets that align with the organization's strategic objectives. The ability to project future financial performance based on historical data and market trends is a valuable skill that can significantly impact an organization's planning and resource allocation.

Tax preparation and compliance are also significant aspects of an accountant's role. This involves preparing tax returns, ensuring compliance with tax laws and regulations, and advising clients on tax planning strategies. The complexity of tax regulations requires accountants to stay updated on changes in tax laws and to interpret and apply these laws accurately. Introverts, who often enjoy deep, focused work and continuous learning, can excel in this area. The solitary nature of tax preparation, combined with the intellectual challenge of navigating complex regulations, makes this aspect of accountancy particularly appealing to introverts.

Forensic accounting is another specialized field within accountancy that offers unique opportunities for introverts. Forensic accountants investigate financial discrepancies and fraud, using their analytical skills to uncover financial misconduct and support legal proceedings. This role requires a high level of attention to detail, critical thinking, and the ability to work independently on complex investigations. Introverts, who often thrive in roles that require deep concentration and methodical problem-solving, can find forensic accounting to be a highly rewarding and intellectually stimulating career path.

Management accounting, also known as cost accounting, focuses on providing financial information to an organization's management team to aid in decision-making. This involves analyzing costs, budgeting, and performance evaluation. Introverts, who often excel in detailed and analytical work, can provide valuable insights that help managers make informed decisions about resource allocation, cost control, and strategic planning. The ability to work closely with management while maintaining a focus on financial analysis makes management accounting an attractive option for introverts seeking a blend of independent work and strategic involvement.

The advancement of technology has significantly transformed the field of accountancy, introducing sophisticated software and tools that streamline financial processes and data analysis. Introverts with a strong aptitude for technology can leverage these tools to enhance their efficiency and accuracy. Proficiency in accounting software, spreadsheet applications, and data analysis tools is essential for modern accountants. The ability to work with these technologies allows introverts to manage large volumes of financial data with precision and to perform complex analyses that inform strategic decision-making.

Furthermore, the rise of data analytics in accountancy has opened new avenues for introverts who enjoy working with data. Data analytics involves the use of statistical and computational techniques to analyze financial data and derive actionable insights. Introverts, who often excel in analytical and methodical tasks, can harness the power of data analytics to uncover trends, identify risks, and optimize financial performance. This integration of data analytics into accountancy not only enhances the value that accountants bring to their organizations but also aligns well with the strengths of introverts who thrive in data-driven environments.

Ethical considerations are paramount in the field of accountancy, as accountants are often entrusted with sensitive financial information. Integrity, confidentiality, and professionalism are core principles that guide the work of accountants. Introverts, who typically value ethical behavior and personal integrity, are well-suited for roles that require a high level of trust and responsibility. The ability to handle confidential information discreetly and to adhere to ethical standards is crucial for maintaining the credibility and trustworthiness of the accounting profession.

Professional development and continuous learning are integral to a successful career in accountancy. Accountants must stay abreast of changes in accounting standards, tax laws, and industry practices. This commitment to lifelong learning aligns well with the intellectual curiosity and self-directed learning preferences of many introverts. Accountants can pursue various certifications, such as Certified Public Accountant (CPA), Certified Management Accountant (CMA), or Certified Internal Auditor (CIA), to enhance their expertise and career prospects. These certifications require rigorous study and examination, providing introverts with the opportunity to engage deeply with their field and achieve professional recognition.

The work environment of an accountant is typically conducive to the preferences of introverts. Many accounting tasks can be performed independently, allowing introverts to work in quiet and focused settings. Whether working in an office, remotely, or in a hybrid arrangement, accountants often have the flexibility to create a work environment that suits their needs. The ability to work independently on detailed tasks, combined with the structured nature of accounting work, enhances job satisfaction and productivity for introverts.

Accountancy also offers diverse career paths and opportunities for specialization. In addition to traditional roles in public accounting firms, accountants can work in corporate finance, government agencies, non-profit organizations, and academia. This diversity allows introverts to find niche areas that align with their interests and strengths, whether it be tax accounting, auditing, financial analysis, or consulting. The ability to choose a specialization that resonates with their preferences and expertise adds to the appeal of a career in accountancy.

Moreover, the demand for accountants is consistently high across various industries, providing job security and career stability. The essential nature of financial management and compliance ensures that skilled accountants are always in demand. This stability, combined with the potential for career advancement and professional growth, makes accountancy an attractive option for introverts seeking a reliable and rewarding career.

Chapter 15: Virtual Assistant

The role of a virtual assistant (VA) has gained significant prominence in recent years, especially as businesses increasingly adopt remote work models and digital solutions. This career offers a multitude of opportunities for introverts who thrive in environments that allow for independent, focused work and minimal face-to-face interaction. Virtual assistants provide administrative, technical, and creative support to businesses and entrepreneurs from remote locations, making it a flexible and versatile career option that aligns well with the strengths and preferences of introverts.

At its core, the job of a virtual assistant involves performing a wide range of tasks to support the daily operations of a business. These tasks can include managing emails, scheduling appointments, handling customer service inquiries, performing data entry, and organizing files. Introverts, who often excel in detailed and methodical work, are well-suited for these responsibilities. The ability to work independently, without the constant interruptions that are common in traditional office settings, allows introverts to focus deeply on their tasks and maintain a high level of productivity.

One of the significant advantages of being a virtual assistant is the flexibility it offers. VAs can often set their own hours and work from any location with an internet connection. This flexibility is particularly appealing to introverts, who may prefer to work in quiet, comfortable environments where they can control their workspaces. Whether it's a home office, a quiet café, or a co-working space, introverts can choose the setting that best suits their needs and preferences. This autonomy over their work environment helps reduce stress and enhances overall job satisfaction.

Virtual assistants are typically responsible for managing communication channels for their clients. This can include handling emails, responding to social media messages, and coordinating with other team members or external partners. While these tasks require strong communication skills, they are often conducted through written mediums rather than face-to-face interactions. Introverts, who often excel in written communication, can effectively manage these responsibilities without the social exhaustion that can come from frequent in-person meetings or phone calls. The ability to communicate clearly and professionally through email, chat, and other digital platforms is a key strength for introverts in this role.

Project management is another critical aspect of a virtual assistant's duties. VAs often help their clients plan, coordinate, and execute various projects, ensuring that deadlines are met, and tasks are completed efficiently. This requires strong organizational skills and the ability to manage multiple priorities simultaneously. Introverts, who are often methodical and detail-oriented, can excel in project management roles. They can create detailed project plans, monitor progress, and provide regular updates to their clients, ensuring that everything stays on track. The ability to work independently on these tasks allows introverts to leverage their strengths in planning and execution.

In addition to administrative tasks, virtual assistants can also provide specialized support in areas such as marketing, graphic design, content creation, and website management. Introverts with specific skills or expertise in these areas can find opportunities to apply their talents in meaningful ways. For example, an introverted VA with a background in graphic design can create marketing materials, social media graphics, and website visuals for their clients. Similarly, a VA with strong writing skills can produce blog posts, newsletters, and other content that helps businesses engage with their audience. These specialized roles allow introverts to focus on tasks that align with their interests and strengths, providing a sense of fulfillment and professional growth.

One of the key benefits of working as a virtual assistant is the opportunity for continuous learning and skill development. The diverse range of tasks that VAs handle means that they are constantly exposed to new challenges and learning opportunities. Introverts, who often enjoy deep, focused learning, can thrive in this environment. They can take advantage of online courses, webinars, and other resources to develop new skills and stay updated on industry trends. This commitment to continuous learning not only enhances their value to clients but also provides a sense of personal and professional growth.

The rise of digital tools and platforms has significantly transformed the way virtual assistants work. Tools such as project management software, customer relationship management (CRM) systems, and communication platforms enable VAs to manage their tasks efficiently and collaborate seamlessly with their clients. Introverts with a strong aptitude for technology can leverage these tools to enhance their productivity and effectiveness. Familiarity with software like Asana, Trello, Slack, Zoom, and Microsoft Office Suite can greatly improve a VA's ability to manage projects, communicate with clients, and organize their work. The ability to work comfortably with digital tools is a significant advantage for introverts in this role.

Moreover, the demand for virtual assistants has been steadily increasing, driven by the growth of remote work and the need for businesses to operate efficiently in a digital environment. This growing demand translates to ample job opportunities and the potential for stable, long-term employment. Introverts seeking a reliable and flexible career can find virtual assistant roles that provide both financial stability and the opportunity to work in a manner that suits their preferences. The ability to choose clients and projects that align with their interests and expertise further enhances job satisfaction and career fulfillment.

The role of a virtual assistant also offers significant potential for career advancement and entrepreneurship. Experienced VAs can choose to specialize in high-demand areas such as executive assistance, digital marketing, or e-commerce management, positioning themselves as experts in their field. Additionally, some VAs may decide to start their own virtual assistant businesses, offering services to multiple clients and potentially hiring and managing other VAs. This entrepreneurial path allows introverts to leverage their skills and experience to build a successful business while maintaining control over their work environment and schedule.

Networking and building relationships with clients are essential aspects of a virtual assistant's career. While introverts may find traditional networking events and large social gatherings challenging, they can effectively build and maintain professional relationships through one-on-one interactions and digital communication. Providing high-quality, reliable service helps VAs establish trust and credibility with their clients, leading to long-term working relationships and referrals. Introverts can use their strong listening and observational skills to understand their clients' needs and deliver personalized, effective support.

Work-life balance is another significant advantage of a career as a virtual assistant. The flexibility to set their own hours and work from preferred locations allows VAs to create a balance that suits their personal and professional lives. This balance is particularly important for introverts, who may need time alone to recharge and avoid burnout. The ability to manage their workload and schedule helps introverts maintain their well-being while delivering high-quality service to their clients.

Chapter 16: Technical Writing

Technical writing is an ideal career choice for introverts due to its emphasis on written communication, meticulous research, and the need for deep concentration, often in a solitary environment. This profession involves creating manuals, guides, documentation, and other types of content that explain complex technical information in a clear, concise, and accessible manner. For introverts who often prefer working independently and excel in environments that require focus and attention to detail, technical writing can be particularly fulfilling.

Technical writing requires a unique blend of skills that cater to an introvert's strengths. One of the primary skills is the ability to understand complex information. Technical writers must have the intellectual curiosity and capability to delve deeply into subjects, whether it's software development, engineering processes, medical procedures, or any other technical field. This involves extensive research, reading, and learning, often done through solitary study, which aligns well with introverts' preference for introspection and deep thinking.

Another crucial aspect of technical writing is the ability to communicate this complex information clearly and effectively. This skill leverages an introvert's strength in written communication. Introverts often excel at articulating their thoughts in writing, as it allows them time to process information and construct their narratives carefully. In technical writing, clarity and precision are paramount. Writers must break down intricate concepts into simple, understandable language without losing the essence of the information. This process requires careful planning and drafting, skills at which introverts typically excel due to their methodical nature and attention to detail.

Technical writing also offers a structured and predictable work environment, which can be very appealing to introverts. Unlike roles that demand constant interaction and spontaneous problem-solving in dynamic settings, technical writing allows for a more controlled and steady workflow. Introverts can often set their own pace, work within established frameworks, and enjoy the process of organizing and synthesizing information without the frequent interruptions that come with more extroverted roles. This level of autonomy and the ability to work in a quiet, uninterrupted setting can significantly enhance job satisfaction for introverts.

Collaboration, while necessary, tends to be more structured and focused in technical writing. Technical writers often work with subject matter experts (SMEs) to gather the necessary information. These interactions are typically well-defined and purposeful, revolving around specific information needs rather than ongoing, spontaneous social engagement. This suits introverts well, as they prefer meaningful and productive interactions over small talk and socializing for its own sake. Moreover, much of the communication with SMEs can be done via email or scheduled meetings, reducing the need for constant in-person interaction and allowing introverts to prepare thoroughly for each exchange.

The career path in technical writing can also be quite flexible and diverse. Technical writers can work in various industries, including technology, healthcare, manufacturing, finance, and more. This diversity allows introverts to choose fields that interest them the most, further enhancing their job satisfaction. Whether working for a tech company producing user manuals and help guides for software applications, or for a healthcare firm creating detailed procedural documentation and regulatory submissions, technical writers have the opportunity to find niches that align with their personal and professional interests.

Moreover, technical writing can often be done remotely, offering even more appeal to introverts. The rise of remote work means that many technical writers can work from home or any quiet location of their choosing. This flexibility reduces the need for daily commuting, provides a comfortable and personalized work environment, and allows for a better work-life balance. Remote work can also minimize workplace social pressures, enabling introverts to focus more on their tasks without the added stress of navigating office dynamics.

In addition to writing skills, technical writers often benefit from a good grasp of technology and various software tools used to create and manage documentation. This might include word processing software, content management systems (CMS), diagramming tools, and more specialized software for creating structured documents. Introverts, who often enjoy learning and mastering new tools independently, can find satisfaction in developing these technical proficiencies. This aspect of the job allows for continuous learning and professional development, which can be very rewarding.

Finally, the impact of a technical writer's work can be very fulfilling for introverts. Knowing that their clear, concise, and well-organized documentation helps users understand and use products effectively can provide a strong sense of accomplishment. Technical writers play a crucial role in enhancing user experience and safety, especially in fields like healthcare and engineering where precise instructions are critical. This sense of contributing to the greater good, while doing work that suits their strengths and preferences, can lead to a highly satisfying career.

Chapter 17: Transcription

Transcription is a highly suitable career for introverts due to its solitary nature and the focus on meticulous detail, allowing for deep concentration and independent work. In essence, transcription involves converting spoken words into written text, and this can cover a wide range of formats, including interviews, lectures, meetings, podcasts, legal proceedings, medical dictations, and more. The job requires excellent listening skills, a strong grasp of grammar and punctuation, and the ability to type quickly and accurately. For introverts who prefer working in quiet environments and enjoy tasks that require precision and focus, transcription can be an ideal career choice.

One of the key aspects that make transcription appealing to introverts is the opportunity to work alone. Transcriptionists often work in quiet settings where they can concentrate without interruptions, which is conducive to the introverted preference for solitude. This kind of work environment minimizes the need for constant interaction with colleagues, clients, or customers, allowing introverts to focus entirely on their tasks. The solitary nature of the job also means that transcriptionists can often work from home, providing a comfortable and personalized workspace that further enhances their productivity and job satisfaction.

The process of transcription is inherently detailed and methodical, aligning well with the strengths of introverts. Transcriptionists must listen carefully to audio recordings and accurately convert them into written text. This requires a high level of concentration and attention to detail, as even minor errors can change the meaning of the transcribed content. Introverts, who are typically thorough and meticulous in their work, excel in such environments where precision is paramount. They can spend extended periods focused on their tasks without the need for social engagement, which can be draining for them.

Furthermore, transcription work allows introverts to leverage their strong listening and comprehension skills. Understanding various accents, speech patterns, and technical terminology is crucial in this field. Introverts often have the patience and dedication needed to repeatedly listen to difficult sections of audio to ensure accuracy. This deep listening skill, combined with their ability to understand context and nuances, makes them well-suited for transcription tasks that require careful interpretation and attention to detail.

Another significant advantage of transcription as a career is the flexibility it offers. Many transcriptionists work as freelancers or independent contractors, giving them control over their schedules. This flexibility allows introverts to structure their work hours in a way that suits their natural rhythms and personal preferences. They can choose to work during times when they feel most productive, whether that's early in the morning, late at night, or any time in between. This autonomy can lead to a better work-life balance and reduce the stress associated with rigid work schedules and constant social interactions.

Transcriptionists can specialize in various fields, providing opportunities to align their work with their interests and expertise. For example, legal transcriptionists convert court hearings, depositions, and legal dictations into written documents, while medical transcriptionists transcribe doctors' notes, patient records, and medical reports. This specialization not only allows introverts to delve deeply into subjects they are passionate about but also opens up opportunities for continual learning and professional growth. The specialized knowledge required in these fields can make the work more engaging and rewarding, as transcriptionists become experts in their chosen areas.

The use of technology in transcription is another factor that makes this career appealing to introverts. Transcriptionists often use various software tools to assist in their work, such as audio playback software, word processing programs, and speech recognition technology. Introverts, who often enjoy working with technology and learning new tools, can find satisfaction in mastering these applications. Additionally, the ability to work independently with these tools without the need for constant human interaction aligns well with their work style preferences.

The demand for transcription services continues to grow, providing a stable and potentially lucrative career path. With the proliferation of digital content, podcasts, online courses, virtual meetings, and the need for accurate documentation in legal and medical fields, the need for skilled transcriptionists is on the rise. This growing demand means that introverts who pursue a career in transcription can find ample job opportunities and the potential for steady income. Moreover, as they gain experience and build a reputation for accuracy and reliability, transcriptionists can command higher rates and secure long-term clients.

In addition to traditional transcription work, there are opportunities in related fields such as captioning and subtitling. Captioners transcribe spoken dialogue for television programs, movies, and online videos, providing a valuable service for the hearing impaired and for viewers who prefer reading along. Subtitlers translate and transcribe foreign language content for films and TV shows, adding another layer of complexity and interest to the work. These related fields allow introverts to further diversify their skills and find niches that match their interests and strengths.

Another aspect of transcription work that appeals to introverts is the low barrier to entry. While specialized fields like legal and medical transcription may require additional training or certification, many transcription jobs simply require good language skills, typing proficiency, and a keen ear. This accessibility makes it possible for introverts to start a career in transcription without extensive upfront investment in education or training. There are numerous online resources, courses, and communities that can help aspiring transcriptionists develop their skills and find job opportunities.

Finally, the intrinsic satisfaction of transcription work should not be underestimated. The act of transforming spoken words into written text can be deeply gratifying for introverts who take pride in their ability to produce clear, accurate, and well-organized documents. The sense of accomplishment that comes from completing a challenging transcription project and knowing that their work will be used and appreciated by others can provide a strong sense of purpose and fulfillment.

Chapter 18: E-commerce

E-commerce, the business of buying and selling goods and services online, is a highly suitable career path for introverts, offering numerous opportunities to leverage their strengths in a predominantly solitary and autonomous work environment. Building and managing online stores involves a wide array of tasks, from designing and developing the website to managing inventory, processing orders, handling customer inquiries, and analyzing sales data. Each of these aspects can cater to the strengths of introverts, making e-commerce an appealing and potentially lucrative career choice.

One of the primary attractions of e-commerce for introverts is the ability to work independently. Introverts often thrive in environments where they can control their own schedules and work without constant interruptions. Running an online store allows them to do just that. They can plan their workday around tasks that require deep focus and concentration, such as developing product listings, optimizing their website for search engines, and analyzing sales metrics. The autonomy of managing an e-commerce business means introverts can create a workspace that is conducive to their productivity, whether that's a quiet home office or a secluded co-working space.

Designing and developing online store taps into the creative and technical skills that many introverts possess. Building a user-friendly and visually appealing website requires a good understanding of web design principles, coding skills, and an eye for detail. Introverts, who often enjoy working with technology and solving complex problems, can find great satisfaction in creating and refining their online store. They can spend hours meticulously crafting each element of their website, from the layout and navigation to the color scheme and typography, ensuring that it not only looks good but also provides a seamless shopping experience for customers.

Managing inventory and processing orders are other key components of running an e-commerce store that suit introverted individuals. These tasks involve tracking stock levels, updating product listings, and ensuring that orders are fulfilled accurately and efficiently. Introverts, who are typically organized and detail-oriented, can excel in these areas. They can set up systems and processes to manage their inventory effectively, minimizing the risk of stockouts or overstocking. Additionally, the process of fulfilling orders can be a solitary activity that allows introverts to work quietly and methodically, ensuring each order is packed and shipped correctly.

Customer service, often seen as a challenge for introverts, can be managed effectively in an e-commerce context with the right strategies. While traditional customer service roles may require constant interaction with customers face-to-face or over the phone, e-commerce customer service can be handled primarily through written communication. Introverts often excel at written communication, which allows them to think carefully about their responses and provide clear, thoughtful answers to customer inquiries. Email support, live chat, and social media interactions are all avenues through which introverts can manage customer service effectively without the stress of constant verbal interactions.

Another significant advantage of e-commerce is the opportunity for introverts to delve into data analysis and optimization. Running a successful online store requires a deep understanding of sales trends, customer behavior, and marketing effectiveness. Introverts, who often enjoy analyzing data and identifying patterns, can use various analytics tools to gather insights about their business. They can track metrics such as website traffic, conversion rates, average order value, and customer retention rates. By interpreting this data, they can make informed decisions about their marketing strategies, product offerings, and website design, continuously optimizing their store for better performance.

The flexibility of e-commerce allows introverts to pursue their passions and interests in a business context. Whether they are passionate about fashion, technology, handmade crafts, or any other niche, they can build an online store around products they genuinely care about. This alignment of personal interests with professional endeavors can lead to higher levels of job satisfaction and motivation. Introverts can immerse themselves in their chosen niche, researching market trends, sourcing products, and creating compelling content that resonates with their target audience.

Moreover, e-commerce offers the potential for scalability, allowing introverts to grow their business at their own pace. Starting with a small, manageable online store, they can gradually expand their product range, increase their marketing efforts, and automate various aspects of their business as they gain more experience and confidence. This gradual approach to growth suits introverts, who may prefer to take their time to ensure everything is running smoothly before scaling up. The ability to automate tasks such as order processing, email marketing, and social media posting also frees up time for introverts to focus on strategic planning and creative endeavors.

E-commerce also provides opportunities for introverts to collaborate in a controlled and structured manner. While introverts may prefer working independently, collaboration is sometimes necessary, especially as the business grows. However, in e-commerce, collaboration can often be done remotely and asynchronously. For example, introverts can work with graphic designers, content creators, and marketing experts via email, project management tools, and video conferencing. These interactions are usually focused and goal-oriented, reducing the need for spontaneous socializing and allowing introverts to prepare for and control their interactions.

Additionally, the global nature of e-commerce means that introverts can operate their business from anywhere in the world. This geographic flexibility allows them to choose a working environment that suits their preferences, whether that's a bustling city or a quiet rural area. The ability to reach a global customer base from the comfort of their own home can be particularly appealing to introverts who value their personal space and autonomy.

The ongoing learning and professional development opportunities in e-commerce also align well with introverted personalities. The e-commerce landscape is constantly evolving, with new technologies, marketing strategies, and consumer behaviors emerging regularly. Introverts, who often enjoy learning and self-improvement, can stay engaged and motivated by keeping up with these changes. They can take online courses, read industry blogs, and participate in webinars to continually enhance their knowledge and skills. This commitment to learning can lead to better business outcomes and personal growth.

Finally, the financial potential of e-commerce cannot be overlooked. While building a successful online store requires hard work and dedication, the potential for significant financial rewards is high. Introverts who are willing to invest the time and effort into building and optimizing their e-commerce business can achieve substantial income and financial independence. The ability to generate passive income through automated systems and repeat customers adds to the financial appeal, providing a stable and potentially scalable source of revenue.

Chapter 19: Content Creation

Content creation, encompassing platforms like YouTube, blogging, and podcasting, represents a compelling career choice for introverts, providing a medium where they can express their creativity, share their knowledge, and engage with an audience on their own terms. Each of these avenues—YouTube, blogging, and podcasting—offers unique opportunities and caters to different strengths and interests, making them highly adaptable to the introverted personality. Let's explore each in detail.

YouTube offers a dynamic platform for introverts who are comfortable with video content creation. Despite its seemingly extroverted nature, YouTube can be an introvert-friendly space when approached thoughtfully. Creating videos allows introverts to plan their content meticulously, script their ideas, and control the production process. Introverts often excel in environments where they can think deeply and organize their thoughts before presenting them, and YouTube provides exactly that opportunity. They can film and edit videos in the solitude of their own space, refining each detail until they are satisfied with the final product.

YouTube channels can cover a vast array of topics, from educational content and tutorials to personal vlogs and artistic endeavors. Introverts can choose niches that align with their passions and expertise, whether it's technology reviews, book recommendations, cooking recipes, or travel guides. By focusing on subjects they are genuinely interested in, introverts can create content that resonates deeply with their audience. Moreover, the visual and auditory elements of YouTube allow for a rich and engaging presentation, which can be particularly appealing for introverts who prefer structured and thoughtful communication over spontaneous interactions.

One of the key advantages of YouTube for introverts is the ability to connect with a global audience while maintaining a degree of separation. Unlike traditional social interactions, engaging with viewers through comments, messages, and social media allows for asynchronous communication. Introverts can take their time to respond thoughtfully to viewer feedback, fostering a sense of community without the pressure of immediate, face-to-face interaction. Additionally, the analytic tools provided by YouTube help introverts understand their audience better, enabling them to tailor their content and improve engagement over time.

Blogging, on the other hand, is a quintessentially introverted pursuit, revolving around the written word. It offers introverts a platform to express their thoughts, ideas, and stories in a controlled and reflective manner. Bloggers can take their time to craft well-thought-out articles, exploring topics in depth and presenting their viewpoints clearly and coherently. This process of writing and editing allows introverts to communicate at their own pace, without the need for spontaneous verbal interaction.

Blogs can cover a multitude of subjects, from personal journals and opinion pieces to in-depth guides and industry analysis. Introverts can find their niche and establish themselves as authorities in their chosen fields. For instance, a blog on sustainable living, tech innovations, literary analysis, or mental health can attract a dedicated readership that values the introvert's unique perspective and expertise. Blogging also provides an opportunity for introverts to engage in research, another activity they often enjoy. They can delve into topics that interest them, gathering information and presenting it in a coherent and informative manner.

The flexibility of blogging is another significant advantage. Introverts can work from any location, at any time, making it an ideal career for those who prefer a flexible and autonomous work environment. They can set their own schedules, balancing their writing with other activities and personal commitments. This level of control over their work environment and routine can significantly enhance job satisfaction and productivity.

Engagement with readers, much like YouTube, can be managed in a way that suits introverts. Comments and social media interactions allow for thoughtful, deliberate communication. Introverts can build a community around their blog, connecting with readers who share their interests and values. This engagement often leads to meaningful and rewarding interactions, which can be deeply fulfilling for introverts who prefer quality over quantity in their social interactions.

Podcasting represents another exciting avenue for introverted content creators, combining the strengths of both YouTube and blogging. Podcasting allows introverts to share their voice and ideas without the need for visual presentation, which can be less daunting for those who are camera-shy. The audio format enables a focus on storytelling, discussion, and in-depth analysis, often appealing to introverts who enjoy deep and meaningful conversations.

Podcasts can cover a wide range of topics, from storytelling and interviews to educational content and niche hobbies. Introverts can choose formats that suit their style, whether it's solo episodes, co-hosted shows, or guest interviews. Solo podcasting allows for complete control over the content and pacing, while co-hosted shows and interviews can provide opportunities for structured and purposeful interactions. The preparation involved in podcasting, from researching topics to scripting and editing, plays to the strengths of introverts who prefer to plan and organize their thoughts.

The production process of podcasting is also conducive to introverted work habits. Recording and editing can be done in a quiet, solitary environment, allowing for concentration and focus. Introverts can take their time to perfect their episodes, ensuring high-quality content that reflects their standards. Additionally, podcasting equipment and software are increasingly accessible, making it easier for introverts to start their own shows with minimal initial investment.

Engagement with the podcast audience follows a similar pattern to YouTube and blogging. Listener feedback through reviews, emails, and social media can be managed asynchronously, giving introverts the space to respond thoughtfully. Building a podcast community can lead to loyal and engaged listeners who appreciate the unique perspective and content provided by the introverted host.

Monetization opportunities across YouTube, blogging, and podcasting also add to their appeal as careers. Content creators can generate income through various means such as advertising, sponsorships, merchandise sales, and crowdfunding. For instance, YouTube offers ad revenue through the Partner Program, while bloggers can monetize their sites through display ads, affiliate marketing, and sponsored posts. Podcasters can attract sponsors, offer premium content through subscription models, and sell branded merchandise. These revenue streams allow introverts to build sustainable careers around their passions and interests, providing financial stability and independence.

Another significant advantage of content creation is the continuous learning and growth it encourages. The digital landscape is ever-evolving, with new platforms, tools, and trends emerging regularly. Introverts, who often enjoy learning and self-improvement, can stay engaged and motivated by keeping up with these changes. They can explore new content formats, experiment with different strategies, and refine their skills over time. This commitment to growth can lead to better content, increased audience engagement, and greater professional satisfaction.

Moreover, the personal and professional connections that content creation can foster are invaluable. Introverts can build relationships with other creators, industry experts, and their audience, often leading to collaborative opportunities and mutual support. These connections, while primarily online, can be deeply meaningful and fulfilling, providing a sense of community and belonging.

Chapter 20: UX/UI Design

UX/UI design, which stands for User Experience and User Interface design, is an exceptional career choice for introverts, offering a blend of creativity, technical skill, and analytical thinking, all within a largely independent and focused work environment. UX/UI designers are responsible for designing the interfaces through which users interact with digital products, ensuring that these interactions are intuitive, efficient, and enjoyable. This role requires a deep understanding of user needs and behaviors, combined with a strong aesthetic sense and technical prowess. For introverts, who often excel in environments that require thoughtful analysis and meticulous attention to detail, UX/UI design can be particularly fulfilling.

One of the most appealing aspects of UX/UI design for introverts is the nature of the work itself. The design process typically involves a great deal of solitary research, planning, and creation. Introverts often thrive in situations where they can focus deeply without constant interruptions. In UX/UI design, this involves conducting user research, analyzing data, creating wireframes, developing prototypes, and refining designs based on user feedback. Each of these tasks allows for periods of uninterrupted concentration, enabling introverts to immerse themselves fully in their work.

User research is a foundational element of UX design that plays to the strengths of introverts. This phase involves gathering and analyzing data on user behaviors, needs, and pain points. Introverts, who often excel in tasks that require careful observation and critical thinking, can find this aspect of the job particularly satisfying. They can conduct surveys, interviews, and usability tests, often remotely or through written communication, minimizing the need for constant face-to-face interaction. Analyzing the data collected allows introverts to draw meaningful insights that inform the design process, ensuring that the final product aligns with user expectations and requirements.

Wireframing and prototyping are other key components of UX/UI design that suit introverted personalities. These tasks involve creating low-fidelity sketches and high-fidelity interactive prototypes that represent the layout and functionality of the digital product. Introverts, who often possess a keen eye for detail and a strong sense of organization, excel in these areas. They can spend hours refining their designs, ensuring that every element is placed thoughtfully and serves a specific purpose. This meticulous approach results in interfaces that are both aesthetically pleasing and highly functional, enhancing the overall user experience.

The iterative nature of the design process also aligns well with introverts' work habits. UX/UI design is a continuous cycle of testing, feedback, and refinement. Introverts, who often prefer to take their time to perfect their work, can appreciate the opportunity to revisit and improve their designs based on user feedback and testing results. This iterative approach not only ensures high-quality outcomes but also allows introverts to engage in deep problem-solving, a task they often find rewarding.

Visual design, an integral part of UI design, taps into the creative talents of introverts. This aspect of the job involves selecting color schemes, typography, iconography, and other visual elements that contribute to the overall look and feel of the product. Introverts, who often have strong visual and artistic sensibilities, can find great satisfaction in this creative aspect of the role. They can experiment with different design elements, explore new trends, and create visually compelling interfaces that attract and retain users.

Collaboration in UX/UI design, while necessary, is typically structured and purposeful, which suits introverts well. Designers often work with product managers, developers, and other stakeholders to ensure that the design aligns with business goals and technical constraints. These interactions are usually well-defined and focused on specific project requirements. Introverts can prepare for meetings, present their ideas clearly, and engage in meaningful discussions about the design. This structured collaboration allows them to contribute effectively without the stress of constant spontaneous interaction.

The rise of remote work has further enhanced the appeal of UX/UI design for introverts. Many design tasks can be performed independently and communicated asynchronously, making it an ideal role for remote work. Introverts can create a comfortable and personalized workspace, free from the distractions and social pressures of a traditional office environment. The flexibility of remote work also allows introverts to structure their workday in a way that suits their natural rhythms, increasing productivity and job satisfaction.

Continuous learning and professional development are key aspects of a career in UX/UI design, which can be particularly appealing to introverts. The field is constantly evolving, with new tools, technologies, and design trends emerging regularly. Introverts, who often enjoy learning and self-improvement, can stay engaged and motivated by keeping up with these changes. They can take online courses, attend webinars, read industry blogs, and participate in design communities to continually enhance their skills and knowledge. This commitment to learning not only leads to better design outcomes but also fosters personal growth and professional advancement.

The impact of UX/UI design on user experience and satisfaction can be deeply fulfilling for introverts. Knowing that their thoughtful and well-crafted designs contribute to a positive user experience can provide a strong sense of accomplishment and purpose. UX/UI designers play a crucial role in creating products that are accessible, user-friendly, and enjoyable to use. This sense of making a meaningful contribution, while doing work that suits their strengths and preferences, can lead to a highly satisfying career.

The diverse range of industries that require UX/UI design expertise also adds to its appeal as a career choice for introverts. Designers can work in technology, healthcare, finance, education, entertainment, and many other sectors. This diversity allows introverts to find niches that align with their interests and values. Whether designing a mobile app for a tech startup, a user interface for medical software, or a website for an educational institution, UX/UI designers have the opportunity to work on projects that they find personally and professionally rewarding.

The potential for freelance work and entrepreneurship in UX/UI design further enhances its attractiveness for introverts. Many designers choose to work as freelancers, offering their services to various clients and enjoying the flexibility and independence that comes with self-employment. Freelance work allows introverts to choose projects that align with their interests, set their own schedules, and work from any location. Additionally, some designers choose to start their own design studios or agencies, providing them with greater control over their work and the ability to build a business around their passion for design.

Chapter 21: Actuarial Science

Actuarial science, a discipline focused on assessing risk and uncertainty using mathematical and statistical methods, is a highly suitable career for introverts, offering a rich blend of analytical precision, intellectual challenge, and solitary work environment. Actuaries play a crucial role in the insurance and finance industries, using their expertise to evaluate the likelihood of future events and devise strategies to minimize financial risk. This career demands a deep understanding of mathematics, statistics, and financial theory, combined with strong problem-solving skills and attention to detail, all of which align well with the strengths of introverted individuals.

One of the primary attractions of actuarial science for introverts is the nature of the work itself, which involves extensive data analysis, model building, and quantitative assessment. Actuaries spend a significant portion of their time working independently, delving into complex datasets, and developing models to predict future events such as mortality rates, illness occurrences, accidents, and natural disasters. This analytical and solitary work environment allows introverts to focus deeply and apply their methodical and meticulous approach to problem-solving.

The process of becoming an actuary involves rigorous education and a series of challenging professional exams, which can be particularly appealing to introverts who enjoy academic pursuits and intellectual challenges. The journey typically begins with a strong foundation in mathematics, statistics, economics, and finance, often acquired through a bachelor's degree in actuarial science or a related field. Introverts, who often excel in academic settings that require concentration and independent study, can thrive in this educational environment. The professional exams, administered by actuarial societies such as the Society of Actuaries (SOA) or the Casualty Actuarial Society (CAS), further enhance the appeal of this career for introverts. These exams require extensive self-study, discipline, and deep understanding of complex concepts, providing a structured and intellectually stimulating path to professional certification.

Actuaries are essential in designing and pricing insurance policies, determining the premiums that customers should pay based on the assessed risks. This task involves creating sophisticated mathematical models that take into account various factors such as age, health status, occupation, lifestyle, and geographic location. Introverts, with their analytical mindset and attention to detail, are well-suited to this type of work. They can meticulously analyze historical data, identify trends, and apply statistical methods to predict future outcomes. The ability to work with complex data and derive meaningful insights is a key strength of many introverts, making them highly effective in this aspect of actuarial science.

Risk assessment and management are core components of actuarial work, requiring actuaries to evaluate potential risks and develop strategies to mitigate them. This involves a thorough understanding of probability theory, financial mathematics, and risk management principles. Introverts, who often have a natural affinity for analytical thinking and problem-solving, can excel in these tasks. They can use their skills to assess the likelihood and impact of various risks, from natural disasters and economic downturns to changes in regulatory environments. By developing strategies to manage these risks, actuaries help organizations safeguard their financial stability and make informed business decisions.

Pension and retirement planning is another significant area where actuaries make a substantial impact. They design and evaluate pension plans, ensuring that these plans are financially sustainable and meet regulatory requirements. This involves calculating future pension liabilities, projecting investment returns, and determining the contributions needed to fund the plans. Introverts, with their methodical approach and precision, can thrive in this work, ensuring that individuals have secure and reliable retirement income. The complexity and long-term nature of pension planning require careful analysis and ongoing monitoring, tasks that align well with the strengths of introverted professionals.

Actuaries also play a crucial role in investment and financial risk management, working with financial institutions to develop and manage investment strategies. They assess the risk and return profiles of various investment options, create diversified portfolios, and monitor market trends to optimize investment performance. Introverts, who often enjoy working with numbers and complex financial concepts, can find this aspect of actuarial science particularly rewarding. Their ability to focus deeply and think critically enables them to develop sound investment strategies that balance risk and return, contributing to the financial health of their organizations.

The collaborative aspects of actuarial work, while necessary, are typically structured and goal-oriented, which suits introverts well. Actuaries often work in teams with other actuaries, financial analysts, underwriters, and business executives to develop comprehensive risk management strategies and financial plans. These interactions are usually focused on specific projects and require clear and concise communication of technical concepts. Introverts can prepare thoroughly for these meetings, presenting their findings and recommendations with confidence. The structured nature of these interactions allows introverts to contribute effectively without the stress of constant spontaneous socializing.

The rise of technology and data analytics has further enhanced the role of actuaries, providing them with advanced tools and techniques to perform their work more efficiently and accurately. Actuaries now use sophisticated software and programming languages such as R, Python, and SQL to analyze large datasets, build predictive models, and automate routine tasks. Introverts, who often enjoy working with technology and complex systems, can leverage these tools to enhance their productivity and effectiveness. The integration of technology in actuarial science allows introverts to focus on higher-level analytical tasks and strategic decision-making, reducing the time spent on repetitive manual calculations.

Continuous professional development is a key aspect of a career in actuarial science, aligning well with the introverted personality. The field is constantly evolving, with new regulations, financial products, and risk factors emerging regularly. Introverts, who often enjoy learning and self-improvement, can stay engaged and motivated by keeping up with these changes. They can participate in professional development courses, attend industry conferences, and read technical journals to continually enhance their knowledge and skills. This commitment to ongoing learning not only ensures that actuaries remain competent and competitive in their field but also fosters personal growth and professional satisfaction.

The financial rewards and job security associated with a career in actuarial science are also significant advantages. Actuaries are among the highest-paid professionals in the financial industry, with strong demand for their skills and expertise. The rigorous education and certification process, combined with the specialized nature of the work, contribute to the high earning potential and job stability in this field. For introverts seeking a financially rewarding career that leverages their analytical strengths and offers long-term security, actuarial science presents a highly attractive option.

Moreover, the diversity of industries that require actuarial expertise adds to its appeal as a career choice for introverts. While traditionally associated with the insurance industry, actuaries are increasingly sought after in healthcare, finance, consulting, and government sectors. This diversity allows introverts to find roles that align with their interests and values. For instance, actuaries working in healthcare can contribute to the design and pricing of health insurance plans, while those in the finance sector can focus on investment risk management and financial planning. This variety of career paths ensures that introverts can find fulfilling roles that match their preferences and strengths.

Chapter 22: Photography

Photography, as a career, offers a unique blend of creativity, technical skill, and personal expression, making it an ideal choice for introverts. It provides an avenue for capturing and interpreting the world quietly and independently. Photographers work in various fields, including portrait, landscape, commercial, and editorial photography, each requiring a distinct set of skills and offering different experiences. For introverts, who often excel in solitary and thoughtful activities, photography presents an opportunity to communicate visually, connect with their environment, and pursue their passion while maintaining their preferred working style.

One of the most appealing aspects of photography for introverts is the autonomy and solitude it often affords. Many photography tasks, such as planning shoots, setting up equipment, and editing photos, can be done independently. This allows introverts to work at their own pace, in their own space, free from the constant social interactions that can be draining. Whether working in a studio or exploring the outdoors for landscape photography, the nature of the work allows introverts to immerse themselves fully in the creative process without the distractions of a busy office environment.

The process of capturing a photograph is both an art and a science, requiring a keen eye for detail, technical knowledge of cameras and lighting, and a deep understanding of composition and visual storytelling. Introverts, who often have a natural affinity for observing and analyzing their surroundings, can excel in this aspect of photography. They can spend time studying the interplay of light and shadow, experimenting with different angles and perspectives, and refining their skills to create compelling images. This meticulous approach to photography allows introverts to produce high-quality work that reflects their unique vision and perspective.

Portrait photography, a popular genre, involves capturing the essence of individuals or groups, often in a controlled studio environment or on location. While this type of photography requires interaction with subjects, introverts can excel by creating a comfortable and relaxed atmosphere. They can use their listening skills and empathy to connect with their subjects, making them feel at ease in front of the camera. This ability to build rapport and trust can result in more authentic and expressive portraits. Additionally, introverts can control the pace and structure of the shoot, allowing them to manage social interactions in a way that feels comfortable and sustainable.

Landscape photography, on the other hand, often involves spending extended periods in natural settings, waiting for the perfect light and weather conditions to capture stunning images of the environment. This genre is particularly well-suited to introverts who enjoy solitude and have a deep appreciation for nature. The patience and perseverance required to capture the beauty of landscapes align well with the introverted personality. They can explore remote locations, observe the changing light, and experiment with different compositions, all while enjoying the peace and tranquility of the natural world.

Commercial photography encompasses a wide range of activities, including product photography, advertising, and corporate photography. This genre requires a strong understanding of visual marketing and the ability to create images that effectively communicate a brand's message. Introverts can thrive in this field by leveraging their analytical skills and attention to detail to produce high-quality, visually appealing images. They can work closely with clients to understand their needs and objectives, then independently plan and execute the shoot to meet those requirements. The structured and project-based nature of commercial photography allows introverts to focus on specific tasks and manage their workload efficiently.

Editorial photography involves creating images for magazines, newspapers, and online publications. This genre often requires a combination of portrait, documentary, and lifestyle photography skills. Introverts can excel in editorial photography by using their ability to tell stories through images. They can work independently to capture compelling visual narratives that complement written content, whether it's a feature article, a fashion spread, or a news story. The opportunity to work on diverse projects and explore different subjects can keep the work interesting and engaging for introverts who enjoy variety and intellectual stimulation.

The post-production process is another aspect of photography that appeals to introverts. Editing photos involves using software such as Adobe Photoshop and Lightroom to enhance and refine images. This task requires concentration, technical skill, and a meticulous eye for detail, all of which are strengths of many introverts. They can spend hours perfecting their images, adjusting colors, contrast, and composition to achieve the desired result. The solitary nature of editing allows introverts to work in a focused and uninterrupted environment, ensuring that the final product meets their high standards.

Photography also offers numerous opportunities for continuous learning and professional development, which can be particularly appealing to introverts who enjoy intellectual growth. The field is constantly evolving, with new technologies, techniques, and trends emerging regularly. Introverts can stay engaged and motivated by taking courses, attending workshops, and participating in photography communities, both online and offline. This commitment to learning not only enhances their skills and knowledge but also keeps their work fresh and innovative.

The financial rewards and flexibility associated with a career in photography are additional benefits that make it attractive to introverts. Photographers can work as freelancers, offering their services to a variety of clients and enjoying the freedom to choose projects that align with their interests and strengths. Freelance work allows introverts to set their own schedules, work from different locations, and maintain a healthy work-life balance. Additionally, photographers can generate income through multiple streams, such as selling prints, licensing images, and offering photography workshops, providing financial stability and independence.

The impact of photography on personal and professional fulfillment can be significant for introverts. Knowing that their images can evoke emotions, tell stories, and capture moments in time can provide a deep sense of satisfaction and purpose. Photography allows introverts to express themselves creatively and share their unique perspective with the world. Whether capturing a fleeting moment of beauty, documenting a significant event, or creating a powerful visual narrative, photographers can make a meaningful contribution to the cultural and artistic landscape.

Furthermore, photography can serve as a therapeutic and meditative practice for introverts. The act of taking photos encourages mindfulness and presence, helping introverts connect with their surroundings and find beauty in the everyday. This mindful approach to photography can reduce stress, enhance well-being, and provide a sense of calm and fulfillment. For introverts who value solitude and reflection, photography offers a way to engage with the world in a meaningful and peaceful manner.

Chapter 23: Medical Coding and Billing

Medical coding and billing are a critical aspect of the healthcare industry, responsible for ensuring that patient care is accurately documented and properly billed. This field requires a high level of precision, attention to detail, and a thorough understanding of medical terminology and healthcare regulations. For introverts, who often excel in roles that demand concentration, analytical thinking, and independent work, medical coding and billing can be an exceptionally rewarding career choice.

The primary responsibility of medical coders is to translate healthcare services, procedures, diagnoses, and equipment into standardized codes. These codes are used for billing purposes and to maintain accurate medical records. This process involves reviewing patient information, including medical histories, lab results, and physician notes, to identify and assign the appropriate codes. Introverts, with their meticulous nature and ability to focus on detailed tasks for extended periods, are well-suited to this type of work. They can work independently, carefully reviewing and coding each document to ensure that it reflects the correct information.

Medical billing, on the other hand, involves submitting and following up on claims with health insurance companies to receive payment for services rendered by healthcare providers. This aspect of the job requires a solid understanding of the billing process, insurance policies, and healthcare regulations. Introverts, who often have strong organizational skills and the ability to manage complex information, can excel in this role. They can handle billing inquiries, resolve discrepancies, and ensure that all claims are processed accurately and efficiently.

One of the most appealing aspects of medical coding and billing for introverts is the potential for remote work. Many healthcare facilities, insurance companies, and billing firms offer remote coding and billing positions, allowing professionals to work from the comfort of their homes. This flexibility provides introverts with a quiet and controlled work environment, free from the distractions and social interactions of a traditional office setting. Remote work also allows for a better work-life balance, enabling introverts to structure their workday in a way that suits their natural rhythms and preferences.

The structured nature of medical coding and billing tasks aligns well with the introverted personality. The work involves clear and defined processes, including reviewing medical records, coding diagnoses and procedures, submitting claims, and following up on unpaid claims. Introverts, who often prefer structured and methodical approaches to their work, can thrive in this environment. They can develop routines and systems that enhance their efficiency and accuracy, leading to high-quality outcomes and job satisfaction.

Accuracy is paramount in medical coding and billing, as errors can lead to denied claims, delayed payments, and potential legal issues. Introverts, who often have a strong attention to detail and a commitment to quality, are well-equipped to handle this responsibility. They can meticulously review each document, cross-reference information, and ensure that all codes are correctly assigned. This careful and precise approach minimizes errors and enhances the overall reliability of the billing process.

The need for confidentiality and discretion in medical coding and billing is another factor that makes it suitable for introverts. Handling sensitive patient information requires a high level of professionalism and respect for privacy. Introverts, who often value privacy and discretion, can manage this responsibility with integrity. They can work quietly and diligently behind the scenes, ensuring that patient data is protected and that all information is handled in accordance with legal and ethical standards.

Continuous learning and professional development are important aspects of a career in medical coding and billing. The field is constantly evolving, with changes in coding systems, healthcare regulations, and insurance policies. Introverts, who often enjoy learning and self-improvement, can stay engaged and motivated by keeping up with these changes. They can pursue certifications, attend workshops, and participate in professional organizations to enhance their skills and knowledge. This commitment to ongoing education not only ensures that they remain competent and competitive in their field but also fosters personal growth and professional advancement.

The potential for career advancement in medical coding and billing adds to its appeal as a career choice for introverts. Experienced coders and billers can move into supervisory or management roles, overseeing teams of coding and billing professionals. They can also specialize in specific areas of coding, such as inpatient or outpatient coding, or pursue roles in auditing, compliance, or education. This career path provides opportunities for introverts to take on leadership roles and contribute to the improvement of coding and billing processes while still working within their preferred environment.

The integration of technology in medical coding and billing has further enhanced the role, providing tools and software that streamline the coding and billing process. Electronic health records (EHR) systems, coding software, and billing platforms enable coders and billers to work more efficiently and accurately. Introverts, who often enjoy working with technology and complex systems, can leverage these tools to enhance their productivity and effectiveness. The use of technology also allows for more remote work opportunities, further aligning with the preferences of introverted professionals.

The financial rewards and job security associated with a career in medical coding and billing are significant advantages. The demand for skilled coding and billing professionals is high, driven by the increasing complexity of healthcare regulations and the need for accurate and efficient billing processes. This demand translates into competitive salaries, job stability, and opportunities for advancement. For introverts seeking a financially rewarding career that leverages their analytical strengths and offers long-term security, medical coding and billing presents a highly attractive option.

Moreover, the impact of medical coding and billing on patient care and the healthcare system can provide a deep sense of fulfillment and purpose. Accurate coding and billing are essential for the financial health of healthcare providers and the overall efficiency of the healthcare system. By ensuring that services are properly documented and billed, coders and billers contribute to the delivery of quality patient care. For introverts who value making a meaningful contribution through their work, this aspect of the role can be particularly rewarding.

Chapter 24: Translation

Translation, the art and science of converting written text from one language into another, is a profession that perfectly aligns with the strengths and preferences of introverts. This career demands a deep understanding of languages, cultural nuances, and context, requiring a meticulous and thoughtful approach to ensure accuracy and maintain the original meaning. For introverts, who often excel in solitary, detail-oriented tasks that involve analytical thinking and precision, translation provides a fulfilling and intellectually stimulating path.

At its core, translation involves more than just substituting words in one language for words in another. It requires a deep comprehension of both the source and target languages, including their grammar, syntax, idioms, and cultural references. Introverts, who often possess strong reading and comprehension skills, are well-suited to this kind of work. They can spend significant time delving into texts, understanding the subtleties of meaning, and ensuring that the translation accurately reflects the original content while being culturally and contextually appropriate for the target audience.

One of the most appealing aspects of translation for introverts is the high degree of autonomy and solitude it offers. Translators typically work independently, spending hours alone with their texts. This environment allows introverts to focus deeply and work without the interruptions and social interactions that can be draining. Whether working from home or in a quiet office, translators can create a workspace that suits their needs, enhancing their productivity and satisfaction.

The process of translation involves several stages, each requiring a high level of attention to detail and analytical thinking. Initially, translators must thoroughly understand the source text, which may involve researching specific terms, concepts, or cultural references. This stage aligns well with the introverted preference for solitary, focused work. Next, the actual translation process requires careful consideration of word choice, tone, and style to ensure that the translated text conveys the same meaning and emotional impact as the original. Finally, the translation must be reviewed and edited to ensure accuracy and consistency, a task that introverts, with their meticulous nature, are particularly adept at.

Specialization within the field of translation can further enhance its appeal to introverts. Translators can choose to focus on areas such as literary translation, technical translation, legal translation, medical translation, or localization. Each specialization offers unique challenges and opportunities for in-depth learning and expertise. For instance, literary translators must capture the nuances and artistic qualities of prose or poetry, requiring a deep appreciation for language and literature. Technical translators, on the other hand, must accurately convey complex information related to fields such as engineering, IT, or science, requiring a strong understanding of technical terminology and concepts. These specialized areas allow introverts to immerse themselves in subjects they are passionate about, combining their love for language with their interest in specific fields.

Translation also offers significant opportunities for continuous learning and professional development, which can be particularly appealing to introverts who enjoy intellectual growth. Languages and cultures are constantly evolving, and translators must stay up-to-date with changes in vocabulary, usage, and cultural trends. Introverts can engage in lifelong learning through advanced language courses, workshops, and professional associations. This commitment to ongoing education not only enhances their skills and knowledge but also keeps their work fresh and engaging.

The use of technology in translation has transformed the profession, offering tools that enhance efficiency and accuracy. Computer-assisted translation (CAT) tools, translation memory software, and machine translation technologies can aid translators in managing large projects, maintaining consistency, and reducing repetitive tasks. Introverts, who often enjoy working with technology and complex systems, can leverage these tools to improve their productivity and focus on the more nuanced aspects of translation. The integration of technology also facilitates remote work, allowing translators to work from anywhere in the world, further aligning with the introverted preference for flexible and autonomous work environments.

Freelance translation is a common career path within the field, offering introverts the ability to control their workload, choose projects that align with their interests, and work from the comfort of their own homes. Freelancers can build a client base, set their own schedules, and create a work environment that suits their needs. This level of autonomy and flexibility is particularly attractive to introverts, who can manage their time and energy effectively, balancing work with personal life.

The impact of translation on global communication and understanding adds a sense of purpose and fulfillment to the profession. Translators play a crucial role in bridging language gaps, enabling people from different cultures to communicate, share knowledge, and collaborate. By translating documents, books, websites, and other materials, translators help to disseminate information, promote cross-cultural understanding, and facilitate international relations. For introverts who value making a meaningful contribution through their work, this aspect of translation can be particularly rewarding.

The financial rewards and job security associated with a career in translation are significant advantages. The demand for skilled translators is high, driven by globalization, international business, and the need for multilingual communication in various sectors. This demand translates into competitive salaries, job stability, and opportunities for career advancement. For introverts seeking a financially rewarding career that leverages their linguistic and analytical strengths, translation presents a highly attractive option.

Furthermore, the potential for travel and cultural immersion is an exciting aspect of a career in translation. Translators who specialize in certain languages or regions may have opportunities to travel for work, attend conferences, or participate in cultural exchange programs. This exposure to different cultures and languages can enrich their personal and professional lives, providing a deeper understanding of the contexts in which they work. For introverts who enjoy solitary travel and cultural exploration, this aspect of translation can add an extra dimension of fulfillment to their careers.

Translation also offers opportunities for collaboration and networking, albeit in a structured and goal-oriented manner that suits introverts. Translators may work with authors, editors, project managers, and other translators on large projects, fostering a sense of community and shared purpose. These interactions are typically focused on specific tasks and outcomes, allowing introverts to engage meaningfully without the stress of constant socializing. Professional associations and online communities also provide platforms for translators to connect, share knowledge, and support each other, further enhancing their professional development and sense of belonging.

Chapter 25: SEO Specialist

An SEO specialist, or Search Engine Optimization specialist, is a professional who focuses on improving a website's visibility on search engines like Google. This role is particularly well-suited for introverts, as it involves a significant amount of independent work, analytical thinking, and strategic planning. It allows individuals to delve deep into the technical aspects of websites, understanding the complex algorithms that search engines use to rank content, and making the necessary adjustments to improve a site's performance in search results.

One of the primary responsibilities of an SEO specialist is keyword research. This involves identifying the terms and phrases that potential customers use when searching for products, services, or information related to the business's offerings. This research is crucial because it forms the foundation of any SEO strategy. By understanding what users are searching for, an SEO specialist can optimize website content to align with these queries, thus improving the chances of the site appearing higher in search engine results pages (SERPs).

Another key aspect of the role is on-page optimization. This involves making sure that each page on a website is set up correctly to attract search engine traffic. On-page optimization includes tasks such as optimizing title tags, meta descriptions, headers, and images, as well as ensuring the content is of high quality and relevant to the target audience. This detailed, methodical work is perfect for introverts, who often excel in tasks that require focus and attention to detail.

Technical SEO is another critical component, which involves optimizing the backend of a website to ensure it meets the technical requirements of search engines. This can include improving site speed, ensuring the site is mobile-friendly, setting up and managing XML sitemaps, and addressing any crawl errors that might be preventing search engines from properly indexing the site. Technical SEO requires a deep understanding of how websites are built and how search engines interact with them, making it an excellent fit for introverts who enjoy diving into the technicalities and solving complex problems.

Link building is also a significant part of an SEO specialist's role. This involves acquiring hyperlinks from other websites to the client's site, which helps to improve its authority and ranking in search engines. While link building does involve some outreach and relationship-building with other webmasters, much of it can be done via email and online communication, making it suitable for introverts who may prefer to avoid extensive face-to-face interaction.

Content creation and strategy form another important aspect of SEO. An SEO specialist must collaborate with content creators to ensure that the content produced is not only engaging and informative but also optimized for search engines. This includes using the right keywords, structuring the content correctly, and ensuring it provides value to readers. Introverts often thrive in environments where they can work independently on creative tasks, making this aspect of the job particularly appealing.

Analytics and reporting are critical to measuring the success of SEO efforts. An SEO specialist must be proficient in using tools like Google Analytics, Google Search Console, and various SEO software to track website performance, understand user behavior, and identify areas for improvement. This involves analyzing data, interpreting trends, and making data-driven decisions to refine and improve SEO strategies. Introverts, who often excel in analytical thinking and prefer working with data over social interactions, may find this part of the job particularly satisfying.

Staying up-to-date with the latest trends and changes in the SEO industry is crucial for success in this field. Search engine algorithms are constantly evolving, and an SEO specialist must continuously educate themselves on new developments, best practices, and emerging tools and techniques. This requires a commitment to ongoing learning and professional development, which many introverts find fulfilling as it allows them to continually improve their skills and knowledge base.

In addition to these specific tasks, an SEO specialist often works closely with other digital marketing professionals, including content writers, web developers, and social media managers, to ensure that the overall digital marketing strategy is cohesive and effective. While this requires some level of collaboration, much of the communication can be done via email, project management tools, and virtual meetings, which may be more comfortable for introverts compared to constant in-person interaction.

Moreover, the nature of the work allows for a high degree of flexibility. Many SEO specialists have the opportunity to work remotely or as freelancers, giving them control over their work environment and schedule. This flexibility can be particularly beneficial for introverts, who may prefer working in a quiet, distraction-free environment where they can focus deeply on their tasks.

Overall, the role of an SEO specialist aligns well with the strengths and preferences of many introverts. It offers a balance of independent work, technical problem-solving, creative content strategy, and data analysis, all of which can be done with minimal direct social interaction. For introverts who enjoy working behind the scenes to make a significant impact on a company's online presence, a career as an SEO specialist can be both rewarding and fulfilling.

Chapter 26: Paralegal Work

A career as a paralegal offers a compelling option for introverts seeking a fulfilling, detail-oriented role that leverages their strengths in research, organization, and written communication. Paralegals play a crucial role in supporting legal teams, handling a variety of tasks that require meticulous attention to detail and a deep understanding of legal procedures and documentation. This profession allows introverts to work in a structured, often quiet environment where they can excel without the need for constant social interaction.

Paralegals are integral to the legal process, performing tasks that range from conducting legal research to drafting documents and managing case files. One of their primary responsibilities is to assist lawyers in preparing for trials, hearings, and corporate meetings. This preparation often involves extensive research into case law, statutes, regulations, and legal articles. Introverts, who are typically adept at focusing on detailed, independent work, are well-suited to this aspect of the job. They can immerse themselves in legal texts and databases, methodically compiling and analyzing information to build strong cases.

In addition to research, paralegals are responsible for drafting legal documents such as contracts, pleadings, and motions. This task requires precision and a strong command of legal terminology and formatting. Introverts often excel in written communication, allowing them to produce high-quality, accurate documents that meet the rigorous standards of the legal profession. Their ability to concentrate deeply and avoid distractions ensures that their work is thorough and reliable.

Managing case files is another critical function of a paralegal. This involves organizing and maintaining a vast array of documents, ensuring that everything is properly filed and easily accessible for attorneys. This organizational aspect of the job plays to the strengths of many introverts, who often have a natural aptitude for creating and maintaining order. The meticulous nature of this work requires someone who is detail-oriented and methodical, qualities that many introverts possess.

Paralegals also play a key role in coordinating and scheduling. They may be responsible for managing the calendars of lawyers, scheduling appointments, depositions, and court dates. This task requires a high degree of organization and the ability to manage multiple tasks simultaneously. Introverts often excel in such roles where they can plan and execute tasks without the need for extensive interpersonal interaction.

Moreover, paralegals are often tasked with communicating with clients, witnesses, and other parties involved in a case. While this may seem challenging for introverts, much of this communication is conducted through written correspondence, emails, and phone calls rather than face-to-face meetings. This allows introverts to engage in necessary interactions in a more controlled and less socially demanding manner.

The role of a paralegal also involves a significant amount of problem-solving. Legal cases often present complex issues that require careful analysis and creative thinking to resolve. Introverts, who are often skilled at deep thinking and analytical reasoning, are well-equipped to handle these challenges. They can take the time to thoroughly understand the nuances of a case, consider all possible angles, and contribute valuable insights to the legal team.

Confidentiality and discretion are paramount in the legal field, and paralegals must adhere to strict ethical standards. Introverts, who are typically trustworthy and conscientious, are naturally suited to handling sensitive information with the required level of confidentiality. Their preference for working independently also reduces the risk of accidental disclosure of confidential information.

The legal field is constantly evolving, and paralegals must stay current with changes in laws and regulations. This requires ongoing education and professional development. Introverts, who often enjoy continuous learning and self-improvement, may find this aspect of the job particularly satisfying. They can take advantage of opportunities to expand their knowledge and skills through courses, seminars, and certifications, thereby enhancing their expertise and value to their legal team.

Another appealing aspect of a paralegal career for introverts is the variety of specializations available within the field. Paralegals can choose to focus on areas such as corporate law, family law, intellectual property, real estate, and criminal law, among others. This allows individuals to find a niche that aligns with their interests and strengths. For example, a paralegal with a keen interest in technology and innovation might specialize in intellectual property law, working on cases related to patents and trademarks. This specialization provides an opportunity to engage deeply with a specific area of law, further enhancing job satisfaction.

Work environments for paralegals can also vary, from large law firms to corporate legal departments, government agencies, and non-profit organizations. This variety offers introverts the flexibility to choose a setting that best suits their preferences. Some may prefer the structured environment of a large firm, while others might thrive in the quieter, more focused atmosphere of a small practice or corporate office.

In addition to traditional employment, many paralegals have the option to work as independent contractors or freelancers. This can provide even greater flexibility and control over their work environment and schedule. For introverts who value autonomy and the ability to work independently, freelancing can be an ideal career path.

The advent of technology has also transformed the paralegal profession, making it even more accessible and suited to introverts.

Many tasks that once required face-to-face interaction can now be completed online, using legal research databases, electronic filing systems, and virtual communication tools. This technological shift allows paralegals to perform their duties with greater efficiency and less direct social interaction, aligning well with the preferences of introverted individuals.

Chapter 27: Database Administration

Database administration (DBA) is a career that is particularly well-suited to introverts due to its emphasis on independent work, technical proficiency, and attention to detail. A database administrator is responsible for managing and maintaining an organization's database systems, ensuring they are efficient, secure, and reliable. This role involves a wide range of tasks that require a deep understanding of database technologies, problem-solving skills, and the ability to work meticulously, all of which align well with the strengths and preferences of many introverts.

At the core of a database administrator's responsibilities is the installation, configuration, and upgrading of database software. This foundational task sets the stage for the database system's performance and reliability. Introverts, who often excel in roles that require careful planning and execution, are well-suited to this aspect of the job. They can work independently, focusing on the intricate details necessary to ensure the software is properly set up and optimized.

Once the database software is installed, a DBA's focus shifts to maintaining and securing the database. This involves regular monitoring and tuning of the database to ensure it operates efficiently. Database performance tuning is a critical task that requires a detailed understanding of the system's architecture and how different components interact. Introverts, who are typically adept at analytical thinking and problem-solving, can excel in this area by methodically analyzing performance metrics and identifying areas for improvement. They can dive deep into the technical aspects of the system, making precise adjustments to enhance performance.

Security is another paramount concern for database administrators. Protecting sensitive data from unauthorized access and breaches is a crucial responsibility. This involves implementing robust security measures such as encryption, access controls, and regular security audits. Introverts often possess a strong sense of responsibility and are naturally vigilant, making them well-suited to maintaining the security of complex information systems. They can meticulously set up and monitor security protocols, ensuring that the data is safeguarded against potential threats.

Backup and recovery are also essential components of database administration. DBAs must ensure that there are reliable backup procedures in place to prevent data loss in case of system failures, corruption, or other disasters. This involves creating and managing backup schedules, testing recovery procedures, and regularly updating backup strategies. The methodical nature of this work suits introverts, who often thrive in roles that require careful planning and contingency management. Their attention to detail ensures that backups are accurate and recovery processes are reliable.

Database administrators are also responsible for managing database user accounts and permissions. This includes setting up new user accounts, defining user roles, and granting or revoking access as needed. This task requires a high level of organization and precision to ensure that users have the appropriate access while maintaining overall system security. Introverts' preference for structured and organized environments helps them excel in managing these user permissions, reducing the risk of unauthorized access or potential security breaches.

Another critical aspect of a DBA's role is ensuring data integrity and quality. This involves implementing data validation procedures, maintaining data consistency across different systems, and ensuring that data is accurately and efficiently stored and retrieved. Introverts often have a keen eye for detail and are highly methodical, which enables them to maintain high standards of data integrity. They can develop and enforce data management policies that ensure the accuracy and reliability of the information stored within the database.

In addition to these technical tasks, database administrators must also be adept at troubleshooting and resolving issues that arise within the database system. This requires a deep understanding of database management systems (DBMS) and the ability to diagnose and fix problems efficiently. Introverts, who are typically persistent and enjoy solving complex problems, are well-equipped to handle these challenges. They can work independently to identify the root cause of issues and implement effective solutions without the need for extensive collaboration or supervision.

Documentation is another important responsibility of a DBA. Maintaining comprehensive documentation of the database system, including configuration settings, backup procedures, security protocols, and user permissions, is crucial for effective database management. Introverts often excel in roles that require detailed documentation and record-keeping. Their ability to focus on detailed tasks ensures that all necessary information is accurately recorded and easily accessible for future reference.

Database administrators also play a key role in the planning and development of new database systems. This involves working closely with other IT professionals, such as developers and system architects, to design databases that meet the organization's needs. While this requires some level of collaboration, much of the planning and development work can be done independently. Introverts, who often prefer to work in a quiet and focused environment, can contribute significantly to the design process by conducting thorough research, analyzing requirements, and developing efficient database solutions.

Continuous learning and professional development are crucial for database administrators, given the rapid pace of technological advancements in the field. DBAs must stay up-to-date with the latest developments in database technologies, security threats, and best practices. Introverts, who often have a strong desire for personal and professional growth, may find this aspect of the job particularly appealing. They can engage in self-directed learning through online courses, certifications, and professional networks, continuously enhancing their skills and knowledge.

Moreover, the role of a database administrator often offers a high degree of flexibility. Many DBAs have the option to work remotely or on a flexible schedule, which can be particularly beneficial for introverts who prefer to work in environments that minimize social interactions and distractions. This flexibility allows them to create a work environment that maximizes their productivity and comfort.

In larger organizations, database administrators may work as part of a team, but even in these settings, there is often a significant amount of independent work involved. DBAs typically have their own areas of responsibility and can focus on their specific tasks without constant supervision. This autonomy aligns well with the preferences of introverts, who often perform best when they have the freedom to work independently and manage their own workload.

Chapter 28: Market Research

Market research is a vital field that involves gathering, analyzing, and interpreting data about markets, consumers, competitors, and the effectiveness of marketing strategies. This career is particularly well-suited for introverts because it requires a significant amount of independent work, analytical thinking, and attention to detail. Introverts often excel in roles that involve deep focus, critical thinking, and methodical analysis, making market research an ideal fit.

At its core, market research aims to understand consumer behavior and preferences to help businesses make informed decisions. This involves a variety of tasks, including designing research studies, collecting data, analyzing results, and presenting findings. Each of these tasks plays to the strengths of introverts, who often prefer working behind the scenes to gather and process information.

One of the primary responsibilities of a market researcher is to design research studies. This involves identifying the objectives of the research, determining the best methods to collect data, and developing detailed plans to ensure that the research is conducted effectively. Introverts often thrive in roles that require careful planning and attention to detail, as they can meticulously outline each step of the research process. This stage also involves creating surveys, questionnaires, and interview guides, which requires a thoughtful and methodical approach to ensure that the questions are clear and will yield valuable data.

Data collection is another crucial aspect of market research. This can involve a variety of methods, including surveys, interviews, focus groups, and observations. While some of these methods, like conducting interviews or moderating focus groups, may involve direct interaction with people, much of the data collection can be done remotely or through online platforms. This allows introverts to gather information without the need for extensive face-to-face communication. Additionally, many market researchers specialize in quantitative methods, such as analyzing online behavior or utilizing existing datasets, which involve minimal social interaction.

Once the data is collected, the next step is data analysis. This involves using statistical tools and software to identify patterns, trends, and insights within the data. Introverts often excel in analytical roles, where they can work independently to interpret complex data sets. This stage of market research requires a high level of concentration and problem-solving skills, as researchers must sift through large amounts of information to find meaningful insights. The ability to work quietly and focus deeply on data analysis makes this aspect of market research particularly appealing to introverts.

After analyzing the data, market researchers must interpret the results and draw conclusions about consumer behavior. This involves synthesizing the findings into clear and actionable insights that can inform business decisions. Introverts often have strong analytical thinking and the ability to see the big picture, allowing them to connect the dots and provide valuable recommendations. They can take the time to thoroughly understand the data and its implications, ensuring that their conclusions are well-founded and reliable.

One of the final steps in the market research process is presenting the findings to stakeholders. While this may seem daunting for introverts, who might prefer to avoid public speaking, there are many ways to share insights without extensive verbal communication. Market researchers often create detailed reports, visual presentations, and dashboards that clearly communicate the results of their studies. Introverts can leverage their strong written communication skills to produce high-quality reports that convey complex information in an understandable and impactful way. Additionally, many presentations can be done virtually or through pre-recorded videos, allowing introverts to present their findings in a more comfortable setting.

Market research also involves a significant amount of secondary research, which entails gathering and analyzing existing data from various sources. This can include reviewing academic journals, industry reports, competitor analysis, and market trends. Introverts, who often enjoy reading and learning independently, are well-suited to this aspect of the job. They can spend time exploring various sources of information, synthesizing the data, and identifying relevant insights that contribute to the overall research objectives.

Another important component of market research is understanding and segmenting the target market. This involves identifying different groups of consumers based on demographics, psychographics, behavior, and other characteristics. Introverts often excel at this type of detailed analysis, as it requires a deep understanding of data and the ability to identify patterns and trends. By segmenting the market, researchers can provide more targeted and effective recommendations to businesses, helping them to better meet the needs and preferences of their customers.

In addition to these core tasks, market researchers must stay up-to-date with the latest trends and developments in their field. This involves continuous learning and professional development, which many introverts find fulfilling. They can attend webinars, read industry publications, and participate in online courses to enhance their skills and knowledge. The rapidly evolving nature of market research means there are always new methodologies, tools, and technologies to explore, providing ongoing opportunities for growth and improvement.

Moreover, market research often offers a high degree of flexibility in terms of work environment and schedule. Many market researchers have the option to work remotely or on a flexible schedule, which can be particularly appealing to introverts who prefer to work in a quiet and controlled environment. This flexibility allows them to create a work setting that maximizes their productivity and comfort, whether they are working from home, in a private office, or in a quiet corner of a library.

Collaboration in market research is typically structured and focused, involving regular but not constant interaction with colleagues and stakeholders. Introverts can thrive in this type of environment, where they can contribute their insights and expertise during scheduled meetings and then return to their independent work. The collaborative aspect of market research allows introverts to share their ideas and receive feedback without the need for continuous social interaction.

In larger organizations, market researchers often work as part of a team, but even within these settings, there is a significant amount of independent work. Each team member may be responsible for different aspects of the research, such as data collection, analysis, or reporting. This division of labor allows introverts to focus on their specific tasks and contribute to the overall project without the need for constant collaboration.

Additionally, market researchers can specialize in various areas, such as consumer behavior, brand research, product development, or advertising effectiveness. This specialization allows individuals to focus on the aspects of market research that most interest them and align with their strengths. For example, an introvert who enjoys data analysis and statistical modeling might specialize in quantitative research, while another who prefers understanding consumer motivations and attitudes might focus on qualitative research.

Technology has also transformed the field of market research, making it even more accessible and suitable for introverts. Advanced data analytics tools, online survey platforms, and social media monitoring tools have streamlined many aspects of the research process. These technologies enable market researchers to collect and analyze data more efficiently, often reducing the need for extensive face-to-face interaction. Introverts can leverage these tools to enhance their productivity and deliver high-quality insights.

Chapter 29: Career Coaching for Introverts

Career coaching is a field that can be incredibly rewarding for introverts, particularly when guiding fellow introverts toward fulfilling careers. Introverts often have a deep well of empathy, strong listening skills, and a preference for meaningful one-on-one interactions. These traits make them particularly suited to helping others navigate their career paths. Career coaching for introverts involves understanding the unique challenges and strengths of introverted clients and guiding them with empathy and insight.

A career coach helps clients identify their career goals, develop job search strategies, improve their resumes and cover letters, prepare for interviews, and navigate career transitions. For introverted clients, a career coach can offer tailored advice that considers their need for quiet, reflective time, and work environments that minimize overstimulation and constant social interaction. This kind of personalized guidance can make a significant difference in helping introverts find careers where they can thrive.

One of the primary roles of a career coach is to listen and understand their client's career aspirations, concerns, and challenges. Introverts are often excellent listeners, which is a critical skill in this profession. They tend to process information deeply and can provide thoughtful, insightful responses. This ability to listen carefully and empathetically allows introverted career coaches to build strong, trusting relationships with their clients. They can create a safe space where clients feel heard and understood, which is especially important for introverts who might struggle with expressing their needs and preferences in more extroverted-dominated environments.

Career coaching for introverts involves helping clients recognize their strengths and how to leverage them in the job market. Introverts often have strong analytical and problem-solving skills, creativity, and the ability to focus deeply on tasks. An introverted career coach can help clients identify these strengths and articulate them effectively on their resumes and during interviews. They can also help clients find roles and work environments that align with their preferences, such as jobs that offer independent work, opportunities for deep focus, and a quiet atmosphere.

In addition to recognizing strengths, introverted career coaches can help clients develop strategies to manage the challenges associated with being an introvert in the workplace. This might include techniques for networking in a way that feels authentic and comfortable, strategies for self-promotion that don't feel overwhelming, and tips for managing energy levels and preventing burnout. For example, they might suggest ways to prepare for networking events, such as researching attendees in advance, setting small goals for the event, and allowing time for recovery afterward.

Another important aspect of career coaching is helping clients set realistic and achievable career goals. Introverted career coaches can guide clients through a process of self-reflection and goal-setting that aligns with their values, interests, and strengths. They can help clients break down their long-term goals into manageable steps, providing support and encouragement along the way. This process often involves helping clients overcome self-doubt and build confidence in their abilities, which is particularly important for introverts who might struggle with self-promotion and visibility.

Career coaches also play a key role in helping clients navigate job searches. This includes assisting with resume and cover letter writing, preparing for interviews, and developing a job search strategy. Introverted career coaches can offer specific advice on how to highlight strengths in a resume or cover letter, such as emphasizing skills like analytical thinking, problem-solving, and creativity. They can also help clients prepare for interviews by practicing responses to common questions, developing strategies for handling difficult questions, and building confidence through mock interviews.

For introverted clients, job search strategies might include focusing on online job search platforms, networking through written communication or small, one-on-one meetings, and leveraging social media to connect with potential employers. Introverted career coaches can help clients identify the best strategies for their personalities and comfort levels, ensuring that they approach their job search in a way that feels authentic and manageable.

Career transitions are another area where introverted career coaches can provide valuable support. Whether clients are changing industries, re-entering the workforce after a break, or seeking a promotion, career coaches can help them navigate these transitions with confidence. This might involve identifying transferable skills, developing a professional development plan, or exploring new career paths that align with their interests and strengths. Introverted career coaches can offer empathetic support and practical advice, helping clients make informed decisions and take proactive steps toward their career goals.

In addition to one-on-one coaching, introverted career coaches might also offer workshops, webinars, and group coaching sessions. These formats can be particularly effective for reaching a broader audience and providing valuable information and support in a more structured setting. For introverts, group coaching sessions can offer a sense of community and shared experience, while workshops and webinars can provide valuable learning opportunities without the need for extensive social interaction. Introverted career coaches can design these sessions to be inclusive and supportive, ensuring that all participants feel comfortable and engaged.

Continuous professional development is important for career coaches, as the job market and career development strategies are constantly evolving. Introverts often have a strong desire for learning and self-improvement, making them well-suited to staying up-to-date with the latest trends and best practices in career coaching. They can attend workshops, read industry publications, and participate in professional networks to enhance their knowledge and skills. This commitment to continuous learning ensures that they can provide the most relevant and effective support to their clients.

Technology has also transformed the field of career coaching, making it more accessible and flexible. Many career coaches offer virtual coaching sessions, which can be particularly beneficial for introverts who prefer to communicate through written or digital means rather than face-to-face meetings. Online platforms allow career coaches to reach clients from all over the world, providing flexibility in scheduling and reducing the need for extensive travel. Introverted career coaches can leverage these technologies to offer high-quality coaching services in a way that aligns with their own preferences and comfort levels.

Moreover, the role of a career coach often offers a high degree of autonomy and flexibility, which can be particularly appealing to introverts. Many career coaches work independently or run their own coaching businesses, allowing them to create a work environment that suits their needs. This autonomy enables them to set their own schedules, choose their clients, and design their coaching programs in a way that aligns with their values and strengths.

Chapter 30: Financial Planning

Financial planning is a career that aligns well with the strengths and preferences of introverts, offering opportunities to work independently, engage in deep analytical thinking, and build meaningful one-on-one relationships with clients. Financial planners help individuals and families manage their finances, plan for the future, and achieve their financial goals. This career requires a high level of expertise, meticulous attention to detail, and the ability to communicate complex financial concepts in a clear and understandable way, all of which are areas where introverts often excel.

At its core, financial planning involves developing comprehensive financial plans that take into account clients' current financial situations, long-term goals, risk tolerance, and personal values. Introverts, who often have strong analytical skills and a preference for thoughtful, detailed work, are well-suited to this aspect of the job. They can spend time thoroughly analyzing clients' financial information, including income, expenses, investments, and debts, to create a detailed picture of their financial health.

One of the primary responsibilities of a financial planner is to help clients set and achieve their financial goals. This process begins with in-depth conversations to understand clients' aspirations, whether they involve buying a home, saving for children's education, planning for retirement, or leaving a legacy. Introverts' natural inclination toward deep, meaningful conversations allows them to connect with clients on a personal level, helping them feel comfortable sharing their financial hopes and concerns. This empathetic approach is crucial in building trust and ensuring that the financial plans they develop are truly aligned with clients' values and objectives.

Once the goals are established, financial planners create tailored strategies to help clients achieve them. This involves selecting appropriate investment vehicles, developing savings plans, and advising on debt management. Introverts often excel in roles that require careful planning and strategic thinking, as they can methodically assess various options and craft personalized plans. They are adept at conducting thorough research and analysis, which is essential for selecting the best investment options and strategies to meet clients' needs.

Risk management is another critical aspect of financial planning. This includes assessing clients' risk tolerance and ensuring their investment portfolios are diversified and aligned with their comfort levels. Introverts' attention to detail and cautious approach are valuable here, as they can meticulously analyze potential risks and develop strategies to mitigate them. They can explain complex concepts such as asset allocation, diversification, and risk-adjusted returns in a way that is easy for clients to understand, helping them make informed decisions about their financial futures.

In addition to investment planning, financial planners often advise clients on tax strategies, retirement planning, estate planning, and insurance needs. These areas require a deep understanding of various financial products and regulations, as well as the ability to stay up-to-date with changes in tax laws and financial markets. Introverts' propensity for continuous learning and their ability to focus deeply on complex subjects make them well-suited to mastering these areas. They can provide clients with expert advice on how to minimize taxes, optimize retirement savings, protect their assets, and ensure their wishes are carried out through proper estate planning.

Effective communication is a crucial skill for financial planners, as they must convey complex financial concepts to clients in a way that is clear and understandable. Introverts often excel in written communication, which can be particularly useful in preparing detailed financial reports, plans, and correspondence. They can also develop strong verbal communication skills, enabling them to explain their recommendations during client meetings. The ability to listen carefully and respond thoughtfully helps introverted financial planners build strong relationships with their clients, ensuring they feel heard and understood.

Financial planners also play a vital role in helping clients navigate life changes and unexpected events. This might include advising on financial implications of marriage, divorce, the birth of a child, or the death of a loved one. Introverts' empathetic nature and ability to provide calm, thoughtful guidance can be particularly valuable during these times of transition. They can help clients adjust their financial plans to reflect their changing circumstances and provide reassurance and support as they navigate these challenges.

Another important aspect of financial planning is ongoing monitoring and adjustment of clients' financial plans. Financial planners must regularly review clients' portfolios, track their progress toward their goals, and make adjustments as needed based on changes in the market or clients' personal situations. Introverts' meticulous attention to detail and methodical approach make them well-suited to this task. They can carefully analyze financial statements, assess investment performance, and identify areas where adjustments are needed to keep clients on track.

Many financial planners work independently or run their own businesses, which can be particularly appealing to introverts who prefer to work autonomously. This allows them to create a work environment that suits their preferences, whether it's a quiet home office or a private space within a larger firm. The flexibility to set their own schedules and manage their own workload is another benefit that can enhance job satisfaction for introverted financial planners.

Technology has also transformed the field of financial planning, making it more accessible and efficient. Financial planning software, online investment platforms, and virtual meeting tools have streamlined many aspects of the job, allowing financial planners to focus more on client relationships and strategic planning. Introverts can leverage these tools to enhance their productivity and provide high-quality service to their clients without the need for extensive face-to-face interaction.

In addition to working with individual clients, financial planners may also work with businesses, helping them develop employee retirement plans, manage corporate investments, and plan for future growth. This aspect of the job can provide additional opportunities for introverts to apply their analytical skills and strategic thinking in a business context. They can help business owners and executives make informed financial decisions that support the long-term success of their companies.

Professional development and continuous learning are important aspects of a career in financial planning. Financial planners must stay up-to-date with changes in financial markets, tax laws, and investment strategies to provide the best advice to their clients. Introverts often have a strong desire for personal and professional growth, making them well-suited to this aspect of the job. They can attend industry conferences, participate in professional organizations, and pursue certifications such as the Certified Financial Planner (CFP) designation to enhance their knowledge and skills.

Networking is an important aspect of building a successful financial planning practice, and while it may seem challenging for introverts, there are ways to approach it that align with their strengths. Introverts can focus on building deep, meaningful relationships with a smaller number of contacts rather than trying to network with a large group. They can leverage their listening skills and thoughtful approach to create lasting connections with clients, colleagues, and other professionals in the industry. Additionally, many networking opportunities are now available online, allowing introverts to connect with others through written communication and virtual meetings.

Chapter 31: Interior Design

Interior design is a field that aligns remarkably well with the strengths and preferences of introverts. This career offers ample opportunities for creative expression, detailed planning, and meaningful one-on-one interactions with clients. Interior designers are responsible for creating aesthetically pleasing, functional, and harmonious spaces within buildings, whether they be homes, offices, hotels, or public spaces. The process of interior design involves a blend of artistic vision, technical knowledge, and practical skills, all of which can be deeply satisfying for introverts who prefer thoughtful, deliberate work.

At the heart of interior design is the creation of spaces that enhance the quality of life and culture of the occupants. This requires a deep understanding of the clients' needs, preferences, and lifestyle. Introverts, who are often keen observers and good listeners, can excel in this aspect of the job. They can engage in meaningful conversations with clients to understand their desires and translate these into design concepts that reflect the clients' personality and style. This ability to listen and empathize helps introverts build strong, trusting relationships with clients, ensuring that the final design is not only beautiful but also highly personalized and functional.

One of the primary responsibilities of an interior designer is to develop a design concept. This involves considering various elements such as color schemes, furniture, lighting, and materials to create a cohesive and aesthetically pleasing space. Introverts often have a keen eye for detail and a strong sense of aesthetics, making them well-suited to this task. They can spend time reflecting on different design ideas, experimenting with color palettes, and exploring various materials to find the perfect combination that brings their vision to life.

The design process also involves creating detailed plans and drawings. This requires technical skills and proficiency in design software, such as AutoCAD, SketchUp, and Adobe Creative Suite.

Introverts often excel in roles that require precision and attention to detail, and they can meticulously create floor plans, elevations, and 3D models that accurately represent the design concept. This aspect of the job allows introverts to work independently, focusing deeply on their work without the need for constant social interaction.

Once the design concept and plans are finalized, interior designers must select and specify materials, furnishings, and accessories. This involves researching products, visiting showrooms, and collaborating with suppliers and vendors. Introverts can leverage their research skills to find the best products that meet the clients' needs and budget. They can also develop strong relationships with suppliers, using their communication skills to negotiate prices and ensure that the products are delivered on time and meet the required standards.

Project management is another crucial aspect of interior design. Designers must oversee the implementation of their design, coordinating with contractors, architects, and other professionals to ensure that the project is completed on time and within budget. While this requires a degree of leadership and coordination, many introverts can excel in this role by using their organizational skills and ability to plan meticulously. They can create detailed project schedules, manage timelines, and ensure that all aspects of the project are executed according to the design specifications.

Interior designers also play a key role in selecting and arranging furniture and accessories. This involves understanding the principles of space planning and ensuring that the furniture layout maximizes both functionality and aesthetics. Introverts often have a strong sense of spatial awareness and can create layouts that enhance the flow and usability of a space. They can also pay close attention to the finishing touches, such as artwork, plants, and decorative items, which add personality and warmth to the space.

Sustainability is becoming an increasingly important consideration in interior design. Designers are often tasked with selecting eco-friendly materials and designing spaces that minimize environmental impact. Introverts, who often have a strong sense of ethics and a desire to make a positive impact, can be particularly passionate about sustainable design. They can stay up-to-date with the latest trends and innovations in green design, ensuring that their projects not only look beautiful but also contribute to the well-being of the planet.

Lighting is another critical element in interior design, as it affects both the functionality and ambiance of a space. Interior designers must understand different types of lighting, including natural light, ambient light, task lighting, and accent lighting, and how to use them effectively. Introverts' attention to detail and ability to focus on the finer points can help them create lighting plans that enhance the mood and usability of a space. They can experiment with different lighting techniques to highlight architectural features, create focal points, and ensure that the space is well-lit for various activities.

Color theory and psychology are also essential components of interior design. Colors can significantly impact the mood and perception of a space, and interior designers must understand how to use color effectively to achieve the desired effect. Introverts often have a deep appreciation for the subtleties of color and can spend time thoughtfully selecting color schemes that enhance the overall design. They can consider factors such as the psychology of color, the interplay of light and color, and how different colors can affect the perception of space and volume.

In addition to residential projects, interior designers may work on commercial spaces, such as offices, retail stores, restaurants, and hotels. These projects often come with unique challenges and requirements, such as adhering to brand identity, ensuring the space is functional for its intended use, and complying with building codes and regulations. Introverts' ability to focus deeply on the details and their strong problem-solving skills make them well-suited to tackle these challenges.

They can create innovative designs that meet the specific needs of commercial clients while also providing an inviting and efficient environment for customers and employees.

One of the benefits of a career in interior design for introverts is the opportunity for flexible work arrangements. Many interior designers work as freelancers or run their own design studios, allowing them to set their own schedules and create a work environment that suits their preferences. This flexibility can be particularly appealing to introverts who thrive in quiet, controlled environments. They can choose to work from a home office, a private studio, or a co-working space, depending on what best supports their productivity and creativity.

Interior design also offers opportunities for continuous learning and professional development. The field is constantly evolving, with new trends, technologies, and materials emerging regularly. Introverts, who often have a strong desire for personal growth and learning, can stay engaged and inspired by attending industry events, participating in workshops, and pursuing advanced certifications. This commitment to continuous improvement ensures that they remain at the forefront of the industry and can offer their clients the most innovative and effective design solutions.

Networking is an important aspect of building a successful interior design career, and while it may seem challenging for introverts, there are ways to approach it that align with their strengths. Introverts can focus on building deep, meaningful relationships with a smaller number of contacts rather than trying to network with a large group. They can leverage their listening skills and thoughtful approach to create lasting connections with clients, colleagues, and other professionals in the industry. Additionally, many networking opportunities are now available online, allowing introverts to connect with others through written communication and virtual meetings.

Technology has also transformed the field of interior design, making it more accessible and efficient. Design software, online mood boards, and virtual reality tools have streamlined many aspects of the job, allowing interior designers to focus more on their creative vision and client relationships. Introverts can leverage these tools to enhance their productivity and provide high-quality service to their clients without the need for extensive face-to-face interaction.

Chapter 32: Quality Assurance

Quality assurance (QA) is an essential component of various industries, ensuring that products and services meet specific standards of quality and reliability. This field is particularly well-suited to introverts, as it requires a high level of attention to detail, analytical thinking, and the ability to work independently. Introverts often excel in roles that involve careful examination, methodical processes, and a focus on continuous improvement. QA professionals play a critical role in maintaining the integrity of products and services, which ultimately leads to customer satisfaction and business success.

At its core, quality assurance involves a systematic process of checking to see whether a product or service being developed is meeting specified requirements. QA aims to improve the development and test processes so that defects do not arise when the product is being developed. This preventive approach contrasts with quality control, which involves identifying and correcting defects after a product has been developed. Introverts' preference for thoughtful, deliberate work aligns well with the QA field's focus on prevention, planning, and process improvement.

One of the primary responsibilities of QA professionals is to develop and implement quality management systems. This involves creating policies, procedures, and guidelines that define the quality standards for the organization. Introverts, who often have strong organizational skills and a meticulous approach to tasks, are well-suited to this aspect of the job. They can develop comprehensive quality management systems that cover every stage of the production or service delivery process, ensuring that quality is built into the system from the start.

Quality assurance also involves conducting audits and inspections to ensure compliance with established standards. QA professionals examine various aspects of the production process, from raw materials and equipment to the final product. Introverts' attention to detail and ability to focus deeply on specific tasks enable them to conduct thorough audits and inspections, identifying potential issues before they become significant problems. They can meticulously review documentation, conduct interviews, and perform on-site inspections to ensure that all aspects of the process meet the required standards.

In addition to audits and inspections, QA professionals are responsible for testing products and services to identify defects and areas for improvement. This involves designing and executing test plans, analyzing test results, and documenting findings. Introverts often excel in roles that require careful analysis and problem-solving skills. They can develop detailed test plans that cover various scenarios and use cases, ensuring that the product or service is thoroughly tested before it reaches the customer. By analyzing test results, they can identify patterns and trends that indicate potential issues, allowing them to recommend corrective actions to improve quality.

Another critical aspect of quality assurance is root cause analysis, which involves identifying the underlying causes of defects and implementing corrective actions to prevent recurrence. This requires a methodical approach and strong analytical skills, both of which are strengths of many introverts. QA professionals can use various tools and techniques, such as the 5 Whys, fishbone diagrams, and failure mode and effects analysis (FMEA), to identify the root causes of quality issues. By addressing these root causes, they can implement lasting solutions that improve the overall quality of the product or service.

Quality assurance professionals also play a vital role in continuous improvement initiatives. This involves regularly reviewing processes and systems to identify opportunities for improvement and implementing changes to enhance quality. Introverts often have a strong desire for continuous learning and improvement, making them well-suited to this aspect of the job. They can conduct research, analyze data, and collaborate with cross-functional teams to identify best practices and implement process improvements. By fostering a culture of continuous improvement, QA professionals help organizations stay competitive and adapt to changing market demands.

Documentation is another crucial component of quality assurance. QA professionals are responsible for creating and maintaining detailed records of quality-related activities, including test plans, audit reports, inspection records, and corrective action plans. Introverts, who often have strong written communication skills, can excel in this aspect of the job. They can produce clear, concise, and accurate documentation that provides a comprehensive record of the quality assurance process. This documentation is essential for demonstrating compliance with regulatory requirements, facilitating audits, and providing a basis for continuous improvement.

Quality assurance also involves training and educating employees about quality standards and best practices. QA professionals develop training programs, conduct workshops, and provide on-the-job training to ensure that all employees understand their role in maintaining quality. Introverts, who often prefer one-on-one or small group interactions, can effectively deliver training in a way that is engaging and informative. They can use their listening skills and empathy to understand employees' concerns and provide tailored guidance and support to help them succeed.

In many industries, quality assurance professionals must stay up-to-date with regulatory requirements and industry standards. This involves regularly reviewing regulations, attending industry conferences, and participating in professional organizations. Introverts, who often have a strong desire for knowledge and expertise, can excel in this aspect of the job. They can stay informed about the latest developments in their field and ensure that their organization's quality management system remains compliant with all relevant requirements.

Technology plays a significant role in quality assurance, with various tools and software available to streamline and automate QA processes. QA professionals must be proficient in using these tools to conduct tests, analyze data, and manage documentation. Introverts, who often have strong technical skills and a preference for working with technology, can leverage these tools to enhance their efficiency and effectiveness. By using technology to automate repetitive tasks and analyze large datasets, QA professionals can focus on higher-level activities that require critical thinking and problem-solving.

Quality assurance is a field that offers a high degree of autonomy and independence, which can be particularly appealing to introverts. Many QA tasks, such as developing test plans, conducting audits, and analyzing data, can be performed independently, allowing introverts to work in a way that suits their preferences. This autonomy enables QA professionals to create a work environment that minimizes distractions and allows them to focus deeply on their tasks.

Networking and collaboration are also important aspects of quality assurance, as QA professionals must work with various stakeholders, including engineers, production managers, suppliers, and customers. While networking may seem challenging for introverts, they can approach it in a way that aligns with their strengths. Introverts can focus on building deep, meaningful relationships with a smaller number of contacts rather than trying to network with a large group. They can leverage their listening skills and thoughtful approach to create lasting connections and effectively collaborate with others.

Continuous professional development is important for QA professionals, as the field is constantly evolving with new technologies, methodologies, and standards. Introverts, who often have a strong desire for personal and professional growth, can stay engaged and inspired by attending industry events, participating in workshops, and pursuing advanced certifications. This commitment to continuous learning ensures that they remain at the forefront of the industry and can offer their organization the most innovative and effective quality assurance solutions.

Chapter 33: Genealogy

Genealogy, the study of tracing family histories, is a field that appeals to many introverts due to its blend of detailed research, solitary work, and meaningful connections with the past and present. This career involves investigating historical records, analyzing genetic information, and building family trees to help individuals understand their ancestry and heritage. Genealogists delve into various sources, such as birth and death certificates, marriage licenses, census records, immigration documents, and even personal letters and diaries, to piece together the intricate puzzle of a family's history.

The process of genealogical research begins with gathering as much information as possible from the client. This involves detailed conversations to learn about family stories, known ancestors, and any existing documentation or photographs. Introverts, who often excel in one-on-one interactions, can create a comfortable and trusting environment where clients feel encouraged to share personal and sometimes sensitive information. These initial discussions are crucial for setting the direction of the research and identifying potential sources of information.

Once the initial information is collected, genealogists embark on the research phase, which requires a high level of focus, attention to detail, and analytical skills. This phase involves sifting through vast amounts of data, including historical records, online databases, and physical archives. Introverts, who typically enjoy solitary, concentrated work, can thrive in this aspect of genealogy. They can spend hours meticulously examining records, cross-referencing information, and verifying facts to ensure the accuracy and reliability of their findings. This detailed and methodical approach is essential for building a credible and comprehensive family history.

Genealogists often use specialized software and online databases to aid in their research. These tools can help organize information, create digital family trees, and access records from various parts of the world. Introverts, who often have strong technical skills and a comfort with using technology, can effectively leverage these tools to enhance their research. They can also stay up-to-date with new developments and resources in the field, continuously improving their methods and expanding their knowledge base.

An important aspect of genealogy is interpreting and contextualizing the information found in historical records. This involves understanding the historical, cultural, and social context in which ancestors lived, as well as recognizing the limitations and biases of historical records. Introverts, who are often deep thinkers and have a strong sense of empathy, can excel in this aspect of genealogy. They can provide insights into how historical events and societal changes might have affected a family's history, offering a richer and more nuanced understanding of the past.

Writing and documentation are crucial components of a genealogist's work. Genealogists must document their research process, findings, and sources meticulously to create a comprehensive and credible family history report. This report often includes narratives that tell the story of the family, complete with genealogical charts and supporting documentation. Introverts, who often have strong writing skills and an appreciation for detail, can produce well-crafted and informative reports that clients can treasure and pass down to future generations. The ability to convey complex information clearly and engagingly is a valuable skill in genealogy, helping to bring the past to life for clients.

In addition to written reports, genealogists may create visual representations of family histories, such as family trees, charts, and timelines. These visual tools can help clients understand their ancestry more intuitively and see connections between different branches of the family. Introverts, who often have a strong sense of aesthetics and attention to detail, can create visually appealing and accurate representations that enhance the overall presentation of the family history.

Genealogists also play a crucial role in helping clients connect with living relatives. This can involve locating distant cousins, reuniting long-lost family members, or facilitating communication between relatives who have lost touch. Introverts, who often excel in building deep, meaningful relationships, can provide compassionate support during these sometimes emotional reunions. They can help clients navigate the complexities of family dynamics and foster a sense of connection and belonging.

DNA testing has become an increasingly important tool in genealogy, offering new ways to explore ancestry and discover genetic connections. Genealogists often assist clients in understanding and interpreting the results of DNA tests, which can reveal information about ethnic origins, genetic traits, and potential relatives. Introverts, who often have strong analytical skills and a preference for working with data, can effectively interpret DNA results and integrate them into the broader context of a family's history. This scientific aspect of genealogy adds another layer of depth to the research, providing clients with a more comprehensive understanding of their heritage.

Genealogy also involves continuous learning and professional development. The field is constantly evolving, with new resources, methodologies, and technologies emerging regularly. Introverts, who often have a strong desire for knowledge and personal growth, can stay engaged and inspired by attending workshops, participating in professional organizations, and pursuing advanced certifications. This commitment to continuous improvement ensures that they remain at the forefront of the field and can offer their clients the most up-to-date and accurate genealogical research.

Many genealogists work as independent consultants or run their own businesses, which can be particularly appealing to introverts who prefer to work autonomously. This allows them to create a work environment that suits their preferences, whether it's a quiet home office or a private research space. The flexibility to set their own schedules and manage their own workload is another benefit that can enhance job satisfaction for introverted genealogists.

Genealogists may also work with institutions such as historical societies, libraries, museums, and archives, contributing their expertise to preserve and interpret historical records. This collaborative work can involve curating exhibits, conducting public outreach, and providing educational programs about genealogy and history. Introverts, who often have a deep appreciation for history and a desire to share their knowledge, can find fulfillment in these roles. They can contribute to the preservation of historical records and help others understand and appreciate their heritage.

Networking is an important aspect of building a successful genealogy career, and while it may seem challenging for introverts, there are ways to approach it that align with their strengths. Introverts can focus on building deep, meaningful relationships with a smaller number of contacts rather than trying to network with a large group. They can leverage their listening skills and thoughtful approach to create lasting connections with clients, colleagues, and other professionals in the field. Additionally, many networking opportunities are now available online, allowing introverts to connect with others through written communication and virtual meetings.

Chapter 34: Event Planning

Event planning is a multifaceted career that involves organizing, coordinating, and managing a wide range of events, from weddings and corporate functions to concerts and festivals. While it might seem at first glance that event planning is a highly extroverted profession due to its social nature, it actually offers many aspects that align well with the strengths and preferences of introverts. Event planners often work behind the scenes, focusing on detailed planning, logistical coordination, and creative problem-solving, which are areas where introverts can excel. This career allows introverts to use their meticulous nature, organizational skills, and ability to work independently or in small, focused teams to create memorable and seamless experiences for clients and attendees.

The process of event planning begins with understanding the client's vision and requirements. Introverts, who are typically good listeners and empathetic communicators, can excel in this initial phase. They can have detailed, one-on-one discussions with clients to gather all necessary information about the event, including the purpose, theme, budget, and specific preferences. This ability to listen and understand the client's needs is crucial for creating a personalized and successful event. Introverts can take the time to delve deeply into the client's vision, ensuring that every detail is captured and considered in the planning process.

Once the initial consultation is complete, the event planner moves into the research and planning phase. This involves finding suitable venues, vendors, and services that align with the client's requirements and budget. Introverts, who often have strong research skills and a keen eye for detail, can thoroughly investigate all options, comparing prices, services, and reviews to ensure the best choices are made. They can spend hours meticulously planning every aspect of the event, from the layout of the venue to the menu selections, ensuring that nothing is overlooked.

Budget management is a critical aspect of event planning. Planners must ensure that the event stays within the allocated budget while still meeting the client's expectations. Introverts, who often excel in analytical and detail-oriented tasks, can manage budgets effectively by keeping meticulous records, negotiating with vendors, and finding creative solutions to stay within financial constraints. This financial acumen is essential for balancing cost and quality, ensuring that the event is both successful and cost-effective.

Event planners are also responsible for coordinating with various vendors, such as caterers, florists, photographers, and entertainment providers. While this requires some degree of social interaction, much of it can be done through emails, phone calls, and scheduled meetings, which can be more manageable for introverts. They can build strong, professional relationships with vendors, using their communication skills to clearly convey expectations and requirements. This behind-the-scenes coordination is crucial for ensuring that all elements of the event come together seamlessly.

Logistical planning is another area where introverts can shine. This involves creating detailed timelines and schedules, arranging transportation and accommodations, and ensuring that all necessary permits and insurance are in place. Introverts' natural inclination for organization and their ability to think critically about potential problems make them well-suited for this aspect of the job. They can anticipate potential issues and develop contingency plans to address them, ensuring that the event runs smoothly even if unexpected challenges arise.

Creative problem-solving is a key component of event planning. Despite careful planning, events often encounter unforeseen issues that require immediate attention and resolution. Introverts, who often excel at thoughtful, analytical thinking, can approach these problems methodically, considering all possible solutions and choosing the best course of action. This ability to remain calm under pressure and think clearly in stressful situations is invaluable in ensuring the success of an event.

On the day of the event, the planner's role shifts to overseeing the execution of all plans and managing the event in real-time. While this can involve some degree of social interaction, much of the work involves behind-the-scenes coordination, ensuring that vendors arrive on time, setups are completed correctly, and any last-minute issues are addressed promptly. Introverts can use their organizational skills and attention to detail to monitor every aspect of the event, ensuring that everything goes according to plan. They can also work closely with a small team of assistants or volunteers, delegating tasks and providing clear instructions to ensure a smooth operation.

Event planning also requires excellent written communication skills. Introverts, who often excel in this area, can create detailed proposals, contracts, and event itineraries that clearly outline all aspects of the event. These documents are crucial for ensuring that all parties involved have a clear understanding of their roles and responsibilities, and they help prevent misunderstandings and errors. Additionally, introverts can use their writing skills to create engaging promotional materials, such as invitations, programs, and social media posts, which are essential for generating interest and attendance.

Technology plays a significant role in modern event planning, and introverts, who often have strong technical skills, can leverage various tools and software to enhance their efficiency and effectiveness. Event management software, project management tools, and digital communication platforms can streamline many aspects of the planning process, allowing introverts to focus on the more strategic and creative elements of their work. These tools can help with everything from budget tracking and vendor management to guest list organization and event promotion.

Networking and professional development are important for building a successful event planning career. While networking may seem challenging for introverts, there are ways to approach it that align with their strengths. Introverts can focus on building deep, meaningful relationships with a smaller number of contacts rather than trying to network with a large group. They can attend industry events, join professional organizations, and participate in online forums and communities to connect with other event planners and vendors. These connections can provide valuable support, inspiration, and opportunities for collaboration.

Continuous learning is also crucial in the ever-evolving field of event planning. Trends, technologies, and best practices are constantly changing, and introverts, who often have a strong desire for personal and professional growth, can stay engaged and inspired by attending workshops, webinars, and conferences. Pursuing advanced certifications and training can also help introverts stay at the forefront of the industry, offering their clients the most innovative and effective event planning solutions.

Event planning offers opportunities for flexibility and autonomy, which can be particularly appealing to introverts. Many event planners work as freelancers or run their own businesses, allowing them to set their own schedules and create a work environment that suits their preferences. This flexibility can help introverts manage their energy levels and create a balance between work and personal life, enhancing their overall job satisfaction and well-being.

Chapter 35: Nonprofit Sector

The nonprofit sector is a diverse and impactful field that offers numerous opportunities for individuals to make a meaningful difference in society. This sector is particularly well-suited for introverts, who often thrive in roles that allow them to work quietly behind the scenes while contributing to causes they are passionate about. Nonprofit organizations encompass a wide range of missions, from humanitarian aid and environmental conservation to education and healthcare. Working in the nonprofit sector can be deeply fulfilling for introverts, as it combines their desire for purposeful work with the ability to utilize their unique strengths, such as analytical thinking, empathy, and attention to detail.

One of the primary roles in the nonprofit sector that suits introverts is that of a grant writer. Grant writers are responsible for researching potential funding sources, writing proposals, and preparing reports to secure funding for the organization. This role requires strong writing skills, attention to detail, and the ability to work independently. Introverts often excel in this type of work, as it involves a significant amount of solitary research and writing. They can delve deeply into understanding the mission and needs of their organization, as well as the priorities and requirements of potential funders. Crafting compelling and persuasive grant proposals allows introverts to contribute to the financial sustainability of the organization, making a significant impact without being in the spotlight.

Another introvert-friendly role in the nonprofit sector is that of a research analyst. Research analysts gather, analyze, and interpret data to support the organization's programs and advocacy efforts. This role involves conducting literature reviews, designing and administering surveys, and analyzing statistical data. Introverts, who often have strong analytical and critical thinking skills, can thrive in this position. They can work independently or in small teams to produce detailed reports and recommendations that inform the organization's strategies and decision-making processes. By providing evidence-based insights, research analysts play a crucial role in helping nonprofits achieve their goals and measure their impact.

Program coordination is another area within the nonprofit sector where introverts can excel. Program coordinators are responsible for planning, implementing, and evaluating specific programs or projects within the organization. This role requires strong organizational skills, attention to detail, and the ability to manage multiple tasks simultaneously. Introverts often possess these qualities and can effectively manage the logistical aspects of program delivery. They can work behind the scenes to ensure that all components of the program are in place, from scheduling and budgeting to coordinating with partners and stakeholders. By ensuring that programs run smoothly and efficiently, program coordinators contribute to the overall success of the organization's mission.

Nonprofit organizations also need skilled individuals to manage their communications and digital presence. Roles such as communications specialist, social media manager, and content creator are ideal for introverts who have strong writing and technical skills. These positions involve creating and curating content for the organization's website, social media platforms, newsletters, and other communication channels. Introverts can use their creativity and attention to detail to craft messages that effectively convey the organization's mission and engage its audience. By working behind the scenes to build the organization's online presence and reputation, they can help attract supporters, donors, and volunteers.

Financial management is another critical area within the nonprofit sector where introverts can make a significant impact. Roles such as accountant, bookkeeper, and financial analyst involve managing the organization's finances, preparing budgets, and ensuring compliance with financial regulations. Introverts, who often have strong analytical and problem-solving skills, can excel in these positions. They can work independently to maintain accurate financial records, analyze financial data, and provide insights that inform the organization's financial strategies. By ensuring the financial health of the organization, they help sustain its operations and enable it to continue its mission-driven work.

Volunteer coordination is a role that combines elements of program management and human resources, making it well-suited for introverts who enjoy organizing and supporting others. Volunteer coordinators are responsible for recruiting, training, and managing volunteers who contribute their time and skills to the organization. While this role does involve interacting with volunteers, much of the work can be done through written communication, such as emails and newsletters, as well as through structured training sessions and meetings. Introverts can use their organizational skills to create comprehensive volunteer programs, develop training materials, and ensure that volunteers have a positive and productive experience. By effectively managing volunteers, they help amplify the organization's impact and reach.

Advocacy and policy work within the nonprofit sector also offer opportunities for introverts to make a difference. Roles such as policy analyst, advocacy coordinator, and legislative liaison involve researching and analyzing policy issues, developing advocacy strategies, and communicating with policymakers and stakeholders. Introverts can excel in these positions by leveraging their analytical and research skills to understand complex policy issues and develop evidence-based recommendations. They can also use their writing skills to craft policy briefs, position papers, and advocacy materials that effectively communicate the organization's positions and priorities. While some aspects of advocacy work may involve public speaking or meetings with policymakers, much of the work can be done through written communication and behind-the-scenes strategy development.

Nonprofit organizations also need effective leaders who can inspire and guide their teams while staying true to the organization's mission and values. Introverts can excel in leadership roles such as executive director, program director, or development director by using their thoughtful and empathetic leadership style. They can build strong relationships with staff, board members, donors, and community partners through one-on-one interactions and small group meetings. Introverts often lead by example, demonstrating integrity, commitment, and a deep understanding of the organization's mission. By fostering a collaborative and inclusive work environment, they can motivate their teams to achieve the organization's goals and create a lasting impact.

Fundraising is another critical function within the nonprofit sector, and introverts can play a key role in developing and implementing fundraising strategies. Roles such as development officer, donor relations manager, and major gifts officer involve cultivating relationships with donors, organizing fundraising events, and managing donor databases. Introverts can excel in these positions by leveraging their strong interpersonal skills to build and maintain meaningful relationships with donors. They can use their writing skills to create compelling fundraising appeals, grant proposals, and stewardship materials. While some aspects of fundraising may involve public speaking or hosting events, introverts can focus on building relationships through personalized communication and thoughtful engagement.

The nonprofit sector also offers opportunities for introverts to contribute to organizational development and capacity building. Roles such as human resources manager, training coordinator, and organizational development consultant involve supporting the growth and effectiveness of the organization and its staff. Introverts can excel in these positions by using their analytical and problem-solving skills to assess organizational needs, develop training programs, and implement best practices in human resources and organizational development. By enhancing the organization's capacity to achieve its mission, they contribute to its long-term sustainability and impact.

Finally, the nonprofit sector provides opportunities for introverts to engage in direct service roles, such as case manager, counselor, and social worker. These roles involve providing support and assistance to individuals and families in need, whether through counseling, advocacy, or resource coordination. Introverts can excel in these positions by using their empathy and listening skills to build trusting relationships with clients and provide personalized support. While these roles do involve direct interaction with clients, the work often takes place in a one-on-one or small group setting, allowing introverts to connect deeply with those they are helping.

Chapter 36: Environmental Science

Environmental science is a multifaceted and critical field dedicated to understanding, protecting, and preserving the natural environment. This discipline involves the study of natural and human-induced processes and their impacts on the Earth's systems. Environmental scientists work to address some of the most pressing issues of our time, such as climate change, pollution, biodiversity loss, and sustainable resource management. For introverts, this field offers a unique blend of solitary research, data analysis, fieldwork, and the opportunity to contribute meaningfully to the well-being of our planet. The various roles within environmental science allow introverts to leverage their analytical skills, attention to detail, and preference for working in quiet, focused settings.

One of the primary roles in environmental science that suits introverts is that of an environmental researcher. Environmental researchers conduct studies to understand environmental problems and develop solutions to mitigate them. This role involves designing and implementing experiments, collecting and analyzing data, and publishing findings in scientific journals. Introverts often excel in this type of work due to their strong analytical and critical thinking skills. They can work independently or in small, focused teams to investigate complex environmental issues. Whether studying the effects of pollutants on ecosystems, analyzing climate data, or researching renewable energy sources, environmental researchers play a crucial role in advancing our understanding of environmental challenges and informing policy decisions.

Fieldwork is a significant component of many environmental science careers, offering introverts the opportunity to engage with nature while conducting valuable research. Field scientists collect samples, monitor environmental conditions, and conduct surveys in various natural settings, from forests and wetlands to oceans and mountains. This hands-on work often involves long periods of solitary or small-group activities, allowing introverts to immerse themselves in their work without the distractions of a busy office environment. The meticulous nature of fieldwork, which requires careful observation, detailed recording, and precise measurements, aligns well with the strengths of introverts.

Environmental modeling is another area within environmental science that is well-suited for introverts. Environmental modelers use computer simulations to predict and analyze environmental changes and their potential impacts. This work involves developing and using mathematical models to simulate processes such as atmospheric circulation, hydrological cycles, and ecosystem dynamics. Introverts, who often have strong technical and problem-solving skills, can excel in this role. They can work independently to develop and refine models, analyze results, and provide insights that can inform environmental management and policy decisions. The ability to focus deeply on complex problems and work with sophisticated software tools makes environmental modeling an attractive option for introverted scientists.

Another important role in environmental science is that of an environmental consultant. Environmental consultants work with businesses, government agencies, and non-profit organizations to assess environmental impacts and develop strategies for sustainable practices. This role involves conducting environmental assessments, preparing reports, and providing recommendations for mitigating negative environmental impacts. While some aspects of this work may involve interacting with clients and stakeholders, much of it can be done through research, data analysis, and report writing. Introverts can use their analytical skills and attention to detail to provide thorough and accurate assessments, helping organizations comply with environmental regulations and improve their sustainability practices.

Environmental science also encompasses conservation biology, a field dedicated to protecting species and their habitats. Conservation biologists study biodiversity, assess threats to wildlife, and develop conservation plans to protect endangered species and ecosystems. This work often involves both field research and laboratory analysis, allowing introverts to engage in a variety of tasks that suit their strengths. Whether tracking animal populations, studying genetic diversity, or developing habitat restoration plans, conservation biologists play a vital role in preserving the planet's biodiversity. Introverts can find fulfillment in this work by contributing to the protection of species and ecosystems and making a tangible difference in the natural world.

Environmental policy and advocacy are other areas where introverts can make a significant impact. Environmental policy analysts and advocates work to shape and promote policies that protect the environment and promote sustainability. This role involves researching and analyzing policy issues, developing policy recommendations, and advocating for environmental protection through written communication and strategic planning. Introverts can excel in these positions by leveraging their strong research and writing skills. They can craft detailed policy briefs, position papers, and advocacy materials that effectively communicate the importance of environmental protection to policymakers and the public. While some aspects of advocacy work may involve public speaking or meetings with stakeholders, much of it can be done through behind-the-scenes work, allowing introverts to contribute to positive change in a way that suits their strengths.

Environmental education and communication are also important components of the environmental science field. Environmental educators and communicators work to raise awareness about environmental issues and promote sustainable behaviors. This role involves developing educational materials, conducting outreach programs, and using various media platforms to disseminate information. Introverts can excel in these positions by using their creativity and communication skills to craft engaging and informative content. Whether developing educational programs for schools, creating informative videos, or writing articles and blog posts, environmental educators and communicators play a crucial role in fostering environmental awareness and encouraging positive action.

Another important role in environmental science is that of an environmental health specialist. Environmental health specialists study the impacts of environmental factors on human health and work to mitigate risks associated with exposure to pollutants and hazardous substances. This role involves conducting research, collecting and analyzing data, and developing strategies to protect public health. Introverts, who often have strong analytical and problem-solving skills, can excel in this work. They can work independently or in small teams to investigate health risks, develop public health guidelines, and provide recommendations for reducing exposure to environmental hazards. By focusing on the intersection of environmental science and public health, environmental health specialists can make a significant impact on both human well-being and environmental protection.

Geospatial analysis is another area within environmental science that is well-suited for introverts. Geospatial analysts use geographic information systems (GIS) and remote sensing technology to analyze spatial data and assess environmental conditions. This work involves mapping and analyzing data related to land use, vegetation cover, water resources, and other environmental factors. Introverts, who often have strong technical skills and attention to detail, can excel in geospatial analysis. They can work independently to develop and interpret maps and spatial data, providing valuable insights for environmental management and planning. The ability to work with sophisticated technology and analyze complex data makes geospatial analysis an attractive option for introverted environmental scientists.

Environmental engineering is another field within environmental science that offers opportunities for introverts. Environmental engineers design and implement solutions to address environmental challenges, such as water and air pollution, waste management, and sustainable resource use. This work involves applying principles of engineering, biology, and chemistry to develop technologies and systems that protect the environment and human health. Introverts can excel in this role by using their problem-solving skills and technical expertise to develop innovative solutions. They can work on designing water treatment systems, developing renewable energy technologies, or creating sustainable waste management practices. The focus on technical problem-solving and the opportunity to work on impactful projects make environmental engineering a rewarding career for introverted individuals.

Chapter 37: Pet Care Services

Pet care services encompass a variety of roles dedicated to the well-being and happiness of animals. These roles range from pet grooming and training to pet sitting and veterinary assistance, each offering unique opportunities for individuals who prefer quieter, more introspective work environments. For introverts, who often find solace and joy in the company of animals, a career in pet care services can be incredibly fulfilling. This field allows introverts to work in a calming environment, engage in meaningful one-on-one interactions, and utilize their attention to detail and empathy, making a significant difference in the lives of pets and their owners.

One of the most common roles in pet care services is that of a pet groomer. Pet groomers are responsible for maintaining the hygiene and appearance of pets, primarily dogs and cats. This role involves bathing, brushing, trimming fur, and clipping nails. Grooming can be a therapeutic activity, both for the groomer and the pet, as it requires patience, gentleness, and meticulous attention to detail—traits often found in introverts. Groomers work in a relatively quiet environment, focusing on one pet at a time, which allows introverts to connect deeply with the animals they care for. The repetitive, hands-on nature of grooming can be calming, providing a sense of accomplishment and satisfaction as the groomer transforms a scruffy pet into a clean and well-groomed companion.

Pet sitting and dog walking are other popular options for introverts interested in pet care services. Pet sitters provide care for pets while their owners are away, ensuring that the animals are fed, exercised, and receive companionship. This role often involves visiting the pet owner's home, which can be less stressful for introverts than a busy workplace. Pet sitters can work independently, following a routine that suits their preferences and the needs of the pets. Similarly, dog walkers take dogs for regular walks, providing essential exercise and socialization.

Walking dogs offers introverts the opportunity to spend time outdoors in a peaceful setting, enjoying the companionship of animals while also getting physical exercise. Both pet sitting and dog walking allow for flexible schedules and the ability to work with minimal supervision, making them ideal for introverts who value autonomy and tranquility.

Pet trainers and behaviorists also play crucial roles in pet care services. These professionals work with pets, primarily dogs, to teach obedience, correct behavioral issues, and provide enrichment. Training requires a deep understanding of animal behavior, as well as patience and consistency—qualities that many introverts possess. Trainers often work in one-on-one sessions with pets, developing customized training plans that address specific issues and goals. This focused, individualized approach allows introverts to build strong bonds with the animals and their owners, providing personalized support and guidance. Working as a pet trainer can be deeply rewarding, as it enables introverts to see the positive impact of their efforts on both the pets and their human companions.

Veterinary technicians and assistants are essential members of the veterinary care team, supporting veterinarians in diagnosing and treating animals. These roles involve a range of tasks, from preparing animals for surgery and conducting laboratory tests to assisting during examinations and providing post-operative care. Introverts often excel in these positions due to their attention to detail, ability to follow precise instructions, and compassionate nature. Veterinary technicians and assistants typically work in a structured environment, such as an animal hospital or clinic, where they can focus on their tasks without constant social interaction. The ability to work closely with animals and contribute to their health and well-being can provide a profound sense of purpose and fulfillment for introverted individuals.

Animal shelters and rescue organizations also offer numerous opportunities for introverts in pet care services. Working in an animal shelter involves caring for homeless, abandoned, or abused animals, helping them recover and find new homes. Roles in shelters can include animal care attendants, adoption counselors, and rehabilitation specialists. Animal care attendants are responsible for feeding, cleaning, and providing basic care for the animals, ensuring they are healthy and comfortable. Adoption counselors work with potential adopters to match them with suitable pets, requiring a balance of interpersonal skills and knowledge of the animals' needs and personalities. Rehabilitation specialists focus on helping animals recover from physical or emotional trauma, providing a safe and nurturing environment. Introverts can thrive in these roles by offering compassionate, individualized care and making a tangible difference in the lives of vulnerable animals.

Pet care services also extend to more specialized roles, such as pet photographers and pet product designers. Pet photographers capture the unique personalities and special moments of pets through photography, creating lasting memories for pet owners. This role allows introverts to combine their love of animals with their creative talents, working in a quiet, focused environment. Pet product designers, on the other hand, develop innovative products that enhance the lives of pets and their owners. This role involves researching, designing, and testing new products, requiring creativity, technical skills, and a deep understanding of animal behavior and needs. Both roles offer introverts the opportunity to work independently and leverage their unique strengths to contribute to the pet care industry.

In addition to these hands-on roles, there are also opportunities for introverts to work in pet care administration and management. Positions such as shelter managers, veterinary practice managers, and pet care business owners involve overseeing operations, managing staff, and ensuring the financial health of the organization. Introverts can excel in these roles by utilizing their organizational skills, attention to detail, and ability to focus on long-term goals. Managing a pet care business or organization allows introverts to create a work environment that aligns with their values and preferences, fostering a culture of compassion and excellence in pet care.

The rise of pet-related technology and services also offers new opportunities for introverts in the pet care sector. Pet tech companies develop apps, devices, and services that enhance pet care and improve the lives of pets and their owners. Roles in this sector can include software developers, product managers, and customer support specialists. Introverts with technical skills can thrive in these positions, working on innovative solutions that address common pet care challenges. Developing pet tech products requires a deep understanding of both technology and animal behavior, allowing introverts to leverage their analytical and problem-solving skills.

Working with animals can also provide therapeutic benefits for introverts. Interacting with pets has been shown to reduce stress, lower blood pressure, and increase feelings of happiness and well-being. For introverts, who may find social interactions draining, spending time with animals can offer a welcome respite and a source of comfort. The bond between humans and animals is unique and powerful, providing introverts with a sense of connection and purpose. By working in pet care services, introverts can experience the joy and fulfillment that comes from helping animals and their owners, while also benefiting from the calming and therapeutic effects of their work.

Chapter 38: Creating a Work-Life Balance

Creating a work-life balance as an introvert involves understanding one's unique needs and preferences to ensure both personal and professional satisfaction. Introverts often require time alone to recharge after social interactions, and maintaining a healthy balance between work responsibilities and personal time is crucial for their well-being. This balance allows introverts to thrive in their careers while also ensuring they have the energy and mental clarity to enjoy their personal lives.

One of the key aspects of achieving work-life balance as an introvert is selecting a career that aligns with one's personality and strengths. Introverts often excel in roles that allow for independent work, deep focus, and minimal social interaction. Careers such as writing, graphic design, data analysis, software development, and research are well-suited for introverts as they often involve solitary work and provide opportunities for deep concentration. By choosing a career that fits their natural inclinations, introverts can reduce stress and enhance job satisfaction, making it easier to maintain a balance between work and personal life.

Setting clear boundaries between work and personal time is another essential strategy for introverts seeking work-life balance. This involves establishing specific work hours and adhering to them, ensuring that work does not encroach on personal time. For those working from home, creating a dedicated workspace can help delineate the boundary between work and leisure. This physical separation can make it easier to switch off from work mode at the end of the day and fully engage in personal activities. Additionally, setting boundaries with colleagues and supervisors regarding availability outside of work hours can prevent work-related interruptions during personal time.

Time management is a crucial skill for maintaining work-life balance. Introverts can benefit from planning their day to include periods of focused work interspersed with breaks to recharge. Techniques such as the Pomodoro Technique, which involves working for a set period followed by a short break, can be effective in maintaining productivity while preventing burnout. Prioritizing tasks and focusing on the most important and time-sensitive ones can help introverts manage their workload efficiently. By staying organized and avoiding last-minute rushes, introverts can reduce stress and ensure they have time for relaxation and personal activities.

Another important aspect of work-life balance for introverts is recognizing and respecting their need for alone time. Introverts recharge through solitude, and ensuring they have enough time alone each day is vital for their mental and emotional well-being. This can involve setting aside time in the morning or evening for activities such as reading, meditating, or simply enjoying a quiet walk. Introverts should also communicate their need for alone time to family members and friends to ensure their personal space is respected.

Developing a supportive work environment is also critical for introverts. This includes creating a workspace that minimizes distractions and allows for focused work. Introverts often prefer quiet environments where they can concentrate without interruptions. For those working in an office, using noise-canceling headphones or finding a quiet corner can help create a more conducive work environment. Employers can support introverted employees by offering flexible work arrangements, such as remote work or flexible hours, allowing introverts to work in an environment that suits their needs.

Maintaining a balance between social interactions and solitude is another key component of work-life balance for introverts. While introverts typically prefer less social interaction, maintaining healthy relationships with colleagues, friends, and family is important. This involves finding a balance between participating in social activities and ensuring enough time for solitude. Introverts can schedule social activities in a way that allows them to recharge in between, ensuring they do not become overwhelmed. It is also helpful for introverts to engage in social activities that they genuinely enjoy and find meaningful, rather than feeling obligated to participate in all social events.

Self-care is an essential practice for introverts seeking work-life balance. This involves taking proactive steps to maintain physical, emotional, and mental well-being. Regular exercise, a healthy diet, and sufficient sleep are foundational to overall health. Additionally, engaging in activities that bring joy and relaxation, such as hobbies, can significantly enhance well-being. Introverts should prioritize self-care activities and treat them as non-negotiable parts of their routine. By taking care of their well-being, introverts can ensure they have the energy and resilience to manage work and personal responsibilities effectively.

Mindfulness and stress management techniques can also be beneficial for introverts striving for work-life balance. Practices such as meditation, deep breathing exercises, and yoga can help introverts manage stress and maintain mental clarity. These practices can be incorporated into the daily routine, providing a way to decompress and recharge. Mindfulness, in particular, can help introverts stay present and focused, reducing anxiety and enhancing overall well-being. By regularly engaging in mindfulness and stress management practices, introverts can improve their ability to cope with the demands of work and personal life.

Introverts can also benefit from building a network of like-minded individuals who understand and respect their need for solitude and quiet time. This network can provide support and encouragement, as well as opportunities for meaningful social interaction. Connecting with other introverts can be particularly helpful, as they are likely to have similar preferences and can offer valuable insights and advice.

Online communities and local groups focused on specific interests or hobbies can be good places to find and connect with like-minded individuals.

Finding a healthy work-life balance as an introvert may also involve periodically reassessing and adjusting one's approach to work and personal life. As circumstances change, such as starting a new job or experiencing significant life events, introverts may need to adapt their strategies to maintain balance. Regularly reflecting on what is working and what needs adjustment can help introverts stay on track and make necessary changes to their routine and boundaries. This proactive approach can prevent burnout and ensure that both work and personal life remain fulfilling and manageable.

Incorporating flexibility into one's routine is another effective strategy for maintaining work-life balance. Life is unpredictable, and having a flexible approach allows introverts to adapt to changing circumstances without becoming overwhelmed. This flexibility can involve adjusting work hours, taking time off when needed, or rearranging personal commitments to accommodate unforeseen events. By maintaining a flexible mindset, introverts can navigate the challenges of work and personal life more effectively.

Employers play a significant role in supporting introverts in their quest for work-life balance. By fostering an inclusive and supportive work culture, employers can help introverted employees thrive. This includes offering flexible work arrangements, recognizing the importance of work-life balance, and providing resources for stress management and mental health. Employers can also create an environment that respects and values different working styles, ensuring that introverts have the space and opportunities to contribute effectively without being forced into extroverted norms.

Finally, it's important for introverts to recognize their achievements and celebrate their successes. Maintaining work-life balance is an ongoing effort, and acknowledging progress can provide motivation and a sense of accomplishment. Whether it's completing a challenging project, sticking to a new routine, or simply taking time for self-care, celebrating these achievements reinforces positive behaviors and contributes to overall well-being.

Chapter 39: Networking Tips for Introverts

Networking is often perceived as a challenge for introverts, who typically prefer smaller, more meaningful interactions over large social gatherings. However, effective networking does not require being extroverted. Instead, introverts can leverage their unique strengths—such as deep listening, thoughtful conversation, and genuine relationship-building—to connect with others in a way that feels authentic and comfortable. Here are some detailed networking tips for introverts to help them build valuable connections their way.

Firstly, it's essential to change the mindset around networking. Introverts often view networking as a daunting task that involves superficial interactions. However, networking can be reframed as an opportunity to build meaningful relationships based on mutual interests and respect. By focusing on the quality of connections rather than the quantity, introverts can approach networking with a more positive and less stressful attitude. Remember, it's about forming genuine connections, not just adding contacts to a list.

Preparation is key for introverts when it comes to networking. Before attending an event or meeting, do some research on the attendees, speakers, or organization. Knowing a bit about the people you are likely to meet can help you feel more confident and provide you with conversation starters. Prepare a few topics or questions related to your interests or the event's theme. This preparation can ease anxiety and help you feel more in control of the situation.

Start small and build your confidence gradually. Introverts might find it easier to begin networking in smaller, more intimate settings rather than large conferences or events. Consider attending smaller meetups, workshops, or professional groups where the atmosphere is more relaxed and less overwhelming. These environments often foster deeper, more meaningful interactions, which are more suited to introverts' preferences.

Leverage your strengths in one-on-one conversations. Introverts excel in deep, meaningful discussions, so focus on engaging in one-on-one or small group interactions rather than trying to work the entire room. When you find someone you'd like to connect with, approach them with a genuine interest in getting to know them. Ask open-ended questions and listen actively. Show that you are genuinely interested in their experiences and perspectives. This approach not only makes the other person feel valued but also helps build a strong foundation for a lasting connection.

Follow up on connections made. Introverts are often great at building rapport during one-on-one interactions but may struggle with maintaining these connections over time. Following up is a crucial step in networking. Send a personalized email or LinkedIn message to the people you meet, referencing something specific you discussed. This reinforces the connection and shows that you value the relationship. Keeping in touch periodically with updates, sharing relevant articles, or congratulating them on their achievements can help maintain and strengthen the relationship over time.

Utilize online networking opportunities. Introverts may find online networking platforms like LinkedIn more comfortable than in-person events. Online platforms allow you to connect with professionals, join groups, participate in discussions, and share your expertise without the pressure of face-to-face interaction. Engage with content by commenting on posts, sharing articles, and sending thoughtful connection requests. This can help you build a professional network at your own pace and comfort level.

Attend events with a purpose. When choosing which networking events to attend, select those that align with your interests and professional goals. This way, you are more likely to meet like-minded individuals with whom you can have meaningful conversations.

Additionally, having a clear purpose for attending an event can make it easier to set goals and stay focused. Whether your goal is to learn something new, meet potential mentors, or explore job opportunities, having a purpose can guide your interactions and make the experience more rewarding.

Find a networking buddy. Partnering with a colleague or friend who is more extroverted can be a great way for introverts to ease into networking events. Your buddy can help initiate conversations and introduce you to others, allowing you to join in more comfortably. Additionally, having someone you know at the event can provide a sense of security and reduce anxiety.

Practice self-care before and after networking events. Networking can be draining for introverts, so it's important to manage your energy levels. Before an event, take some time to relax and recharge. Engage in activities that you find calming, such as reading, meditating, or taking a walk. After the event, give yourself time to unwind and process the experience. Reflect on the positive interactions you had and the connections you made. This self-care routine can help you manage the stress associated with networking and maintain your well-being.

Seek out roles that align with your networking style. Some professional roles involve more networking than others. If networking is a significant part of your job, look for ways to incorporate your preferred style. For example, if you are in a sales or business development role, focus on building deep, long-term relationships with a few key clients rather than trying to connect with everyone. If you work in a collaborative team environment, suggest smaller, focused meetings where you can contribute more effectively. Aligning your role with your networking style can help you perform better and enjoy your work more.

Join professional organizations and communities. Professional associations and online communities related to your field can provide valuable networking opportunities in a more structured and less intimidating environment. These groups often offer forums, webinars, and small group discussions where you can engage with peers and industry experts. Participating in these groups can help you stay informed about industry trends, gain new insights, and connect with professionals who share your interests.

Leverage your existing network. Don't overlook the power of your current connections. Reach out to colleagues, classmates, or friends who can introduce you to others in their network. These warm introductions can be less stressful and more productive than cold networking. Additionally, reconnecting with people you already know can help you re-establish relationships and open new doors.

Focus on adding value. One of the most effective ways to build meaningful connections is to offer value to others. Think about how you can help the people you meet, whether by sharing your expertise, providing resources, or making introductions. When you approach networking with a mindset of giving rather than just taking, you build trust and goodwill. This approach aligns well with the introvert's preference for meaningful interactions and can lead to stronger, more genuine connections.

Develop a personal brand. Establishing a personal brand can make networking easier for introverts. A strong personal brand communicates your expertise, values, and professional identity, helping others understand who you are and what you stand for. You can build your personal brand through blogging, speaking at conferences, participating in panels, or sharing your knowledge on social media. When people are aware of your brand, they are more likely to approach you, reducing the pressure on you to initiate every interaction.

Attend industry conferences and workshops. While large events can be overwhelming, they also offer numerous opportunities to learn and connect. Focus on attending sessions that interest you and take advantage of smaller breakout groups and workshops. These settings are often more conducive to in-depth discussions and can provide valuable networking opportunities. Prepare questions and insights related to the topics discussed, as this can help you engage more confidently with speakers and fellow attendees.

Practice and refine your networking skills. Like any other skill, networking improves with practice. Start with low-pressure environments and gradually challenge yourself with larger events. Reflect on your experiences, identify what worked well, and make adjustments as needed. Over time, you'll develop a networking style that feels natural and effective.

Chapter 40: Continuous Learning

Continuous learning is a fundamental aspect of career development, particularly for introverts who may thrive in environments that value deep thinking, focused study, and independent exploration. In today's rapidly changing job market, staying relevant and evolving in your career requires a commitment to lifelong learning. This commitment not only helps you keep up with industry trends and technological advancements but also enhances your skills, making you more adaptable and valuable in your professional field. For introverts, continuous learning can be an especially enriching experience, allowing them to leverage their natural strengths and preferences to achieve sustained career growth.

One of the primary reasons continuous learning is essential for career development is the pace at which industries are evolving. Technological advancements, shifts in market demands, and emerging trends constantly reshape the professional landscape. By engaging in continuous learning, introverts can stay ahead of these changes, ensuring they remain competitive and relevant in their fields. This proactive approach involves seeking out new knowledge and skills that align with industry developments and anticipating future trends to position oneself advantageously.

Introverts often excel in learning environments that emphasize independent study and deep concentration. Online courses, webinars, and self-paced learning modules are particularly suited to introverts, allowing them to engage with new material at their own pace and in their preferred environment. Platforms like Coursera, edX, and LinkedIn Learning offer a wide range of courses across various fields, enabling introverts to pursue topics of interest without the pressure of traditional classroom settings. These resources provide flexibility, allowing learners to balance their educational pursuits with professional and personal commitments.

Reading is another powerful tool for continuous learning, and it aligns well with introverts' strengths. Whether it's books, industry journals, research papers, or blogs, reading allows introverts to absorb information in a quiet and focused manner. Regular reading can deepen one's understanding of complex subjects, introduce new perspectives, and keep one updated on the latest developments in their field. Creating a dedicated reading list or setting aside specific times for reading can help introverts integrate this practice into their daily routine.

Participation in professional development programs and workshops can also be beneficial for introverts. These programs often provide in-depth knowledge on specific topics and offer opportunities for hands-on learning. Workshops, in particular, tend to be smaller and more interactive, allowing for more meaningful engagement and discussion. Introverts can choose workshops that align with their interests and career goals, ensuring they derive maximum benefit from these experiences.

Networking, while traditionally viewed as an extroverted activity, can be approached in a way that leverages continuous learning for introverts. Engaging in professional associations, attending industry conferences, and joining online forums or discussion groups can provide valuable learning opportunities. These settings allow introverts to connect with peers, mentors, and industry leaders, facilitating the exchange of knowledge and ideas. For introverts, it can be helpful to focus on smaller, more intimate networking events where deep, meaningful conversations are more likely to occur.

Mentorship is another avenue through which introverts can engage in continuous learning. Having a mentor provides access to the wisdom and experience of someone who has navigated similar career paths. Mentors can offer guidance, share insights, and provide feedback, helping introverts to grow professionally. For introverts, one-on-one mentorship relationships can be particularly effective, allowing for focused and personalized interactions that cater to their learning style.

Engaging in projects and taking on new challenges within one's current role can also foster continuous learning. Introverts can seek out opportunities to work on special projects, lead initiatives, or collaborate with colleagues from different departments. These experiences can broaden their skill set, expose them to new areas of their field, and enhance their problem-solving abilities. By stepping out of their comfort zone in a structured and manageable way, introverts can gain valuable experience and demonstrate their capacity for growth and innovation.

Another strategy for continuous learning is to pursue formal education, such as advanced degrees or professional certifications. These credentials can enhance one's expertise, open up new career opportunities, and provide a structured framework for learning. For introverts, the academic environment can be particularly appealing, as it often emphasizes individual study, research, and critical thinking. Pursuing further education demonstrates a commitment to personal and professional development, making one a more attractive candidate for advancement within their field.

Staying curious and cultivating a growth mindset is crucial for continuous learning. Introverts can benefit from embracing a mindset that values learning as an ongoing process rather than a finite goal. This involves being open to new experiences, seeking feedback, and viewing challenges as opportunities for growth. A growth mindset encourages resilience, adaptability, and a willingness to take risks—qualities that are essential for navigating the complexities of today's professional landscape.

Incorporating reflection into the learning process can also enhance its effectiveness. Introverts can set aside time regularly to reflect on what they have learned, how it applies to their work, and what areas they need to explore further. Journaling, for instance, can be a useful tool for capturing insights, tracking progress, and setting future learning goals. Reflective practices help consolidate knowledge, deepen understanding, and provide a sense of direction and purpose in one's learning journey.

Employers also play a significant role in supporting continuous learning. Organizations that value and invest in employee development create an environment conducive to lifelong learning. Introverts can advocate for their learning needs by seeking out employers who offer professional development opportunities, such as training programs, workshops, and tuition reimbursement. Additionally, introverts can take advantage of any learning resources provided by their employer, such as access to online courses, industry conferences, or in-house training sessions.

Balancing continuous learning with other responsibilities requires effective time management. Introverts can create a structured plan that allocates specific time blocks for learning activities, ensuring that it becomes a regular part of their routine. This plan should consider personal preferences and energy levels, allowing for optimal focus and productivity. By integrating learning into their daily schedule, introverts can make steady progress without feeling overwhelmed.

Continuous learning also involves staying informed about industry news and trends. Introverts can subscribe to newsletters, follow thought leaders on social media, and join professional groups to stay updated on the latest developments in their field. This ongoing engagement with industry trends helps introverts anticipate changes, identify opportunities, and make informed decisions about their career path.

Creating a supportive learning environment at home or in the workplace can enhance the continuous learning process. Introverts can set up a dedicated learning space that is free from distractions and conducive to concentration. This space can include necessary resources, such as books, a computer, and a comfortable seating arrangement, to create an inviting and productive learning environment.

In addition to these strategies, introverts can also explore creative outlets that contribute to continuous learning. Engaging in activities such as writing, drawing, or music can stimulate cognitive function, enhance problem-solving skills, and provide a sense of accomplishment. These creative pursuits can complement more formal learning activities, offering a balanced and holistic approach to personal and professional development.

The End.

www.ingramcontent.com/pod-product-compliance
Lightning Source LLC
Chambersburg PA
CBHW020955160726

47994CB00006B/2227